THE NEW WEALTH OF NATIONS

THE NEW WEALTH
OF NATIONS

Surjit S. Bhalla

**SIMON &
SCHUSTER**

London · New York · Sydney · Toronto · New Delhi

A CBS COMPANY

For my parents and Ravinder's
Thank you for emphasizing the need for an education
and for treating daughters and sons equally

CONTENTS

1. The Times Are Changing   1

2. Education–Globalization and Its Confounding Contents   13

3. As the World Turns: From Colonialism to Freedom   29

4. Progress: Lost in 480 Years, Gained in 48 Years   45

5. The Education–Income Connection   59

6. Education As Wealth   71

7. Unlimited Supply of Skilled Labour (USSL):   87
   Causes and Consequences

8. The Future is Women: Women and Transformation   111

9. Education Makes the World Equal   127

10. Poverty is Old, Basic Income is New   141

11. Education: The Driver of the Middle Class   153

12. Education and the Democratization of the Elite   171

13. You Can't Fool Mother Nature   181

    Notes   188
    Select Bibliography   195
    Acknowledgements   204

1

The Times Are Changing

Come writers and critics
Who prophesize with your pen
And keep your eyes wide
The chance won't come again
And don't speak too soon

. . .

For the times they are a-changin'

—The Times They Are A-Changin' *by* Bob Dylan
(*music and lyrics by* Bob Dylan, The Times They Are A-Changin', 1964)

The 1960s should be remembered, will be remembered, and are remembered for the revolution they ushered in our thinking, in our music, and in our attitudes. World War II was over, and globalization was ascendant. Within two decades, the revolution gained pace. And it happened so fast. What happened, and why, is the story behind this book.

What happened? Recall that the Western world (including Japan) was fast recovering from the wars and depression of the previous thirty years. In these countries, per capita incomes expanded at a scorching 4.1 per cent per annum pace between 1951 and 1970. The welfare of the 700 million richest people was expanding, and expanding fast. The developing world (all countries outside of the West and the Soviet Union) housed 2.6 billion poor people in 1970 and their incomes had increased at a paltry 2.3 per cent per annum.

And then it happened. Starting around 1980, the transformation in the world, and in the lives of the poor, has been nothing short of radical, huge, and unprecedented. Over the last thirty-six years (1981–2016), the rich population has expanded its incomes at a 1.4 per cent rate; the poor world rate of expansion of income— 4.1 per cent per annum. The Industrial Revolution has been rightly considered transformative for the Western world; but any objective analysis must surely conclude that transforming the lives of more than 80 per cent of the world's population, within merely thirty to forty years, is a much greater milestone. The intent here is not to compare but rather to illustrate. We must recognize and applaud that what we have just witnessed is the mother of all transformations.

In the iconic 1967 movie *The Graduate*, Benjamin (Dustin Hoffman) returns home from college and at a dinner party hosted in his honour gets pulled aside by Mr McGuire. Mr McGuire tells Benjamin, 'I just want to say one word to you, just one word.'

Nervously, Benjamin says, 'Yes, sir.'

'Are you listening?'

'Yes, Sir.'

'Plastics. There is a great future in plastics.' And so ended one of the most quotable 20 seconds in film history.

What has made this revolution possible? In a word, education. In two words, human capital. In a sentence—the catch-up of the East with the West in terms of schooling, and therefore earning skills, and therefore incomes, which has ultimately resulted in an improvement in world inequality. This process is nowhere near complete. In some countries like South Korea, Singapore, Hong Kong, and China, it can be rightly said that the process has reached a more advanced stage than in others like India, Bangladesh, and Pakistan. And as inexorable progress does take place, the world will have less poor, and become more equal. By 2030, *world* inequality will be the lowest it has been since the (relatively) halcyon days of the mid-19th century, i.e., the lowest ever.

I do not mean to argue or imply that human capital is the whole story. Critics have a tendency to latch on to broad statements and then say, 'But not so in Timbuktu'. Of course, there are other important causal influencers of growth, of catch-up and of poverty reduction. The fortunes of the citizens of a nation are affected by the political environment and political leadership. For a long time it was believed that East Asian economies grew faster because they did not have democracies to shackle them. That 'wisdom' was soon withdrawn when it was documented that most of the African and Latin American economies were growing very slowly owing to the fact that these two continents had the largest share of dictatorships. But strong leadership matters a great deal—witness communist China under Mao Zedong and authoritarian China under Deng Xiaoping (and his successors).

Explaining incomes: Education

Agreed that a Revolution is an emotive and extensive issue, and hence demands far more than just a uni-causal explanation, but some causes are more equal than others. And in this regard the cause of education towers over most of the competition. By far, the most profound effect on income is that of human capital. And to think that the queen (why the queen and not the king is explored in Chapter 8, i.e., a changing social order requires 'she' to have an equal standing with 'he') of social sciences (economics) had missed this transformative cause until as late as the late 1950s! It was then that the genius of Gary Becker—a Nobel laureate from the University of Chicago—unleashed on to the world his all-encompassing treatise on family, fertility, and most importantly (not least for this book), how labour earnings would evolve in the future.

One other important aspect of global education is that it has not all been good news, especially for the losers. The 'losers' are individuals in the West, and the loss is in terms of income *growth*. Economic growth in the developed world has slowed over the last couple of decades, and 'secular stagnation' is how a leading US economist, Lawrence Summers, has described it. This stagnation means that there is now an ever-widening gap between the *aspirations* of the Western middle class and a now emerged *reality*. No longer is the future road paved with healthy growth.

For the last decade or so, the educated workforce in the West is caught, ironically, in a problem that plagued the illiterate East not so long ago. The educated workforce meets Sir Arthur Lewis, another Nobel laureate, and one of the economic geniuses of the 20th century. In an influential article written in 1954, Sir Arthur Lewis outlined why the wages of the unskilled, uneducated worker in the East (aka developing economies or emerging markets) would not rise, and would stay stuck at a constant, minimum, subsistence level.

Marry Sir Arthur with Gary Becker and what do you get? The misfortune of the college-educated Western skilled worker and the increasing fortune of the college-educated worker in the East. In a poignant and ironical twist, the reality today (and which explains much of the recent past and the next decade or two) is the reality of 'Unlimited Supply of Skilled Labour' (sometimes referred to as USSL). It is this phenomenon that explains why labour incomes in the West have been reduced to a trickle from a trot—and hence, why the educated Western worker feels the pain. Also, why world inequality has declined and will continue declining. Score one for global education.

There are several radical implications of this expansion in education and the transformation it is making possible. For centuries, make that since Adam and Eve, men have ruled the world. This dominance is changing, and is directly linked to the expansion of girl's education. Just look at the following numbers; across the world, women constituted less than 25 per cent of the world's population attending college in 1900; in 1980, this percentage was 41 per cent; in 2014, the fraction had risen to around 48.7 percent.[1]

This is a clear indication of increasing equality, and men losing further ground in the future. Score two for global education.

Today you obtain education, tomorrow you conquer the workplace, day after the corporate boardrooms, and on the fourth day, the political landscape. This is happening, and is happening now. As discussed in Chapters 5 and 8, there are several unintended, but hugely positive, consequences of this expansion, equalization, and emerging superiority of women in the educated workplace. There is first the obvious (post-Becker) benefit of population control, an important ingredient in the crucial battle against climate change. More educated women have fewer children, period. Fewer children mean better educated children and a lower carbon footprint. A second and a less appreciated consequence will be a decline in violence, as men commit most (more than 90 per cent) crimes, and domestic violence will decline as the woman becomes an equal, if not the dominant member of the family. A lower carbon footprint and less domestic violence. Score three and four for global education.

There are other important fallouts from this radical transformation, from the emergence and reality of USSL. There are some policymakers in the developing world who, unfortunately, have not grasped this most profound and penetrating side effect of global education—the structural decline of inflation in the world (see Chapter 7 for details).[2] There is many a monetarist being found six feet under because he failed to see the connection—when there is a glut of skilled workers whose wages cannot rise, how can there be inflation? Remember, inflation is a sustained rise in the price level—a very large component of the cost of production is the cost of labour (remember Marx?). And if this cost is stable and flat, how can you have a sustained rise in inflation? Score a major five for the globalization of education.

Should one worry about wealth inequality?

If the income inequality discussion were not enough (and perhaps because world inequality trends do not justify the anguish), the enlightened world has moved towards a concern about wealth inequality. It is believed, and estimates prove so, that more than half of the world's wealth is in the hands of the top 1 per cent (Chapter 6; Credit Suisse [2016]).

But let us step back from shock and awe. Though I was a latecomer to economics, an important part of my education in post-Becker economics was that education was the determinant of income for most individuals, say above 99 per cent. Education, or human capital, was wealth; one invested in education in the early years, and derived a flow of income from this investment in later years. How different is it from wealth owned in the form of shares of a firm, or deposits in a bank? But strangely, the Credit Suisse and other proliferating wealth indices (Wealth-X, Forbes, etc.) do *not* include any portion of the wealth embodied in education. Land, yes. Machinery, yes. But not human capital. A beginning towards a rectification of this error of omission is attempted in Chapter 6, and the results are shockingly enlightening. In 2016, developing countries owned about 40 per cent of the total educational wealth in the world, conservatively estimated at US $330 trillion in 2016. The financial wealth in the world, as estimated by Credit Suisse, was US $256 trillion in 2016. More equal education wealth exceeding very unequal financial wealth? Yes. Score a major six for education.

Along with concern about increased inequality in the West, is the interest in and disbelief over the increasing number of billionaires in the East. This actually forms a large part of the implicit argument against globalization. The 'logic' is: 'Look at these poor countries, with abject poverty.' Yet the capitalist system is tolerating an uncomfortable increase in the number of billionaires (generally men, and generally considered, possibly not inaccurately, playboys). This perception reveals a superficial understanding of the importance of *size*—the size of the population that is. If dollar incomes are going up for the poor, then why not also for the rich? And with each rise in average dollar incomes, the fraction (and number) of millionaires and billionaires increases.

The number of billionaires has to do with the tails of distribution, and the tails are relatively unaffected by the rest of the distribution. Two factors explain the rise in the number of billionaires in the East: first, average per capita incomes have increased threefold since 1980; second, size. Even a very small constant percentage in the tail can lead to a large increase in the number. Indeed, the number of billionaires in most parts of the world can be explained by the rise in the fraction of individuals with college attendance (see Chapter 6).

A matter of size: China and India

You must be wondering: more than halfway through the introduction, and still no mention of the middle class, and little mention of China and India? This book would not have been possible without referring to these two population giants. There are many reasons why the two countries need to be discussed jointly— together they house about 40 per cent of the world's population. It takes 171 out of 204 countries to match India's population, while it takes only three more to match China's. The cupboard of globalization is bare without the content—40 per cent of the world's population today, and in another ten years, 40 per cent of the world's income—in the hands of these two country giants. Time to rectify that anomaly.

The general story is of education as 'the great transformer'; the foot soldiers are the populations of developing economies, particularly China and India. The global transformation would not be as revolutionary if it were not for this *size* phenomenon. In 1980, the combined population of China and India was 1.7 billion, slightly more than half the population in the East. It is this population that has seen the largest strides in higher education, in per capita incomes, and in the growth of the middle class.

These two nations have been alike in so many other ways that they are better classified as 'twins separated at birth'. We will have occasion to discuss this in much greater detail as we move further ahead in this book. At this point, it is important to recognize the following fact, and difference. The twins are not identical and have chosen distinctly different paths to development. India, a democracy, grew at the same rate as China for hundreds of years prior to 1980, a fact explored in some detail in Chapter 3. Since 1980, communist China has grown at a much faster pace than India, though India has also markedly accelerated its growth. The future might just have India catching up with the large ahistorical gap in the per capita incomes of the twins.

An overview of the middle class

Back to the present—what is the middle class? How does one define it, and what are its contours, and why does it matter? In an unpublished manuscript written more than a decade ago for the Peterson Institute for International Economics (PIIE), I had discussed in some detail the measurement and historical importance of the middle class. The title of the manuscript was *Second among Equals: The Middle Class Kingdoms of India and China*, May 2007 (hereafter, sometimes referred to as SAE). Subsequent to that work, there has been a burgeoning of interest in the middle class. As of 2005, when I started work on the *Middle Class* project, there were only 761,000 mentions, ever, of the middle class in publications (Google Scholar); by 2016, this number had jumped to 1.24 million. Chapter 11 contains a quick summary of this literature, and in addition, contains details about the nature, size, and influence of the middle class on policy and development.

As almost definitionally expected, there is a strong relationship in the East between the magnitude of the middle class (at least as defined by us) and the magnitude of college attendees. In many ways, expansion of tertiary (college) education is a *sine qua non* for the expansion of the middle class. The size of the middle class matters for policymaking, and matters for growth. One ignores it at one's own peril. We won't make that mistake—and therefore Chapter 11 is devoted to this exploration and analysis. Score seven for global education.

There is another important fallout of this global expansion in education and the middle class. This change parallels the change in control (from men to women), discussed in detail in Chapter 8. There is an additional transformation—it is the changing of the guard at the helm of affairs—the elite. First, it was the feudal elite that ruled the masses, then came the industrial elite, and later the corporate elite. In this almost seamless transition, the same individuals held power—mostly white, upper class, well-educated men. There are two transitions happening around the world. The first involves the gradual shift in power from men to women; the second not so gradual and more emphatic change is the shift in power from the Westernized upper class elite to the domestic middle class elite. This change is discussed in general, and in particular for India, in Chapter 12. Score eight for global education.

Chapter 13 takes a step back to applaud the telling force of education. It has transformed so much, and mostly for the better. When it has allowed a segment of the population to go astray (as with a lack of respect for the forces of nature), Mother Nature has taught, and will teach, us a lesson. In many (mostly positive) ways the force of education has changed the world for the better—it has improved the lot of the poor and the downtrodden, and has altered (or is altering) the relationship between the peoples and sexes of the world. There isn't a more sweeping force than Mother Nature.

2

Education–Globalization and Its Confounding Contents

There's been some hard feelings here
About some words that were said
. . .

There's been some strange goin's on
And some folks have come and gone
. . .

Remember: one man's ceiling
Is another man's floor

— One Man's Ceiling Is Another Man's Floor *by* Paul Simon
(*music and lyrics by* Paul Simon, There Goes Rhymin' Simon, 1973)

Globalization is news. A decade ago, it was the flavour of the century. Growth was good, greed was good, and both were near universal. Today, the West is in despair, and the Rest are in the midst of a celebration. The West is naturally asking: when will the good days return? This chapter looks at this new divergence; education–globalization may be the force behind this development, and we will attempt a deep dive into its confounding contents.

But before that, here's a brief reminder of what has happened in the *world* over the last few decades (and is still happening). While there will be occasion later to discuss individual countries (especially those which comprise the Western world, China, and India), at present, note the emphasis on the word 'world' in the previous sentence. Simply put, the world never had it so good. To which, the obvious riposte is—why the angst then? Why do we see despair today in the West[3]—a set of countries that have had all odds in their favour for at least the past 300 years? These countries contain, both on average, and in totality, the richest people in the world. But there is genuine concern in these populations about their present, their recent past, as well as their foreseeable future.

There is a one-to-one correspondence—call it a mirror image—between the image of the West today and the image of the Rest fifty years ago. Back then, the Rest contained mass poverty, and it is not relative poverty that is being discussed here. It's absolute, dirt poor poverty—more than half the population in the developing world was less-than-one-dollar-a-day poor. Today, that percentage is in single digits. Surely, the world is a much better place for more than a billion individuals now who are no longer poor.

Globalization: A timeline

In 1200, the selling price of silk in Italy was only three times the selling price of silk in distant China. That was globalization 800 years ago—horses for travel, and the human spirit for roaming, and discovery, and resettlement, and trade. This was the essence of globalization.

While dates are difficult to establish, and controversial, there is a near consensus that, at a minimum, the pace of globalization changed around the year 1980. It is well known that trade and migration—the two components of globalization—have occurred, and at an increasing pace, for centuries. But circa 1980 is a breakout point, and hence a marker for the new beginning.

The past thirty-plus years have seen the most progress in human history, where 'most' refers to the magnitude of people and the intensity (rate of growth). Think of the multiplication of both as the force of change, and once you do, you will recognize that the surge of globalization has never ever been greater—not even close. In case we are in awe of change, here is a sobering thought: in 2015, the price of lentils (as necessary to the Indian diet as bread is to Western diets) for consumers was two-and-a-half times the price paid by the wholesaler, and more than three times that obtained by the farmer. The Rest has plenty of catch-up left.

Advances of globalization have led to a backlash—protests against globalization, which started around the turn of the 21st century (as this book will show, that's not a coincidence), have intensified and are at their peak at this moment. One of the big questions is whether this peak will be seen as a plateau a decade hence.

Every social, political, and economic change creates upheavals. The first lesson in the study of political economy is that there are winners and losers. Noisemaking is almost the exclusive domain of the losers, naturally. It's also expected, because what else will the losers do except hope that their protests help 'fix' their losses.

If we go back a couple of decades, to the mid-90s, world growth was good, and stock markets were high, so much so that Fed Chairman Alan Greenspan declared that we were in an era of irrational exuberance. US growth and markets continued to defy the warnings; between 1986 and 2000, per capita world growth averaged 1.5 per cent per annum, economically one of the best periods in history. The per capita growth rate in the next sixteen years, between 2001 and 2016, was 2.3 per cent, which was even higher.[4] There were no protests about rising inequality then, or about how the top 1 per cent had more than 99 per cent (sic) of the world's wealth.

Why were no protests held in the 1980s and 1990s? Because the influential elite was benefitting from low prices of high-end consumer goods, made possible by the 'poor' workers in the East. Walmart was expanding, and Western consumers were splurging. Inflation was low (one of the most profound and long-lasting effects of globalization) and interest rates were lower.

So why protest now? Because *per capita* growth in the Western world—the prime domain—has stuttered, and sputtered, and has proceeded at a snail's pace—with only a 0.7 per cent rate of growth between 2001 and 2016. That is one-fourth the rate of growth in the previous fifty years (1951–2000). The situation is worse because, as pointed out by Piketty and others, a large share of this paltry one-fourth growth has accrued to the top 1 or, at best, the top 5 per cent.[5]

In sharp contrast, the poor countries began their long march towards catch-up post-1980. A reversal of historical misfortune began in earnest. The poor economies registered a growth rate double that experienced by the rich countries—3 per cent per annum compared to the rich countries which grew at 1.5 per cent per annum which, needless to say, was considerably slower than their earlier pace. And the two poorest countries, India and China, saw their incomes increase at an even faster pace—above 5.8 per cent per annum for thirty-six years (1980 to 2016).

This miracle has never occurred before, i.e., when about a billion people (about 350 million poor in India and 650 million poor in China in 1980) increase their incomes by 700 per cent in a short space of just thirty-six years. One can, of course, debate how much of this increase in the incomes of the poor countries was caused by globalization.

The rapid decline in world poverty has been only, and entirely, made possible by the forces of globalization. These forces have disproportionately benefitted the poor, the middle class, and the rich in the developing world. Why this disproportion? Because of catch-up—the workers in developing countries were behind the curve, and in the process of catching up, grew faster.

But globalization has its costs, though in a reversal of the Industrial Revolution days, it is the 'core' (the Western world; the periphery is the East) that is losing from globalization. In the first phase of this globalization (let us call it 1980–2000), it is likely that the working class in the developed world lost out to the blue-collar workers in the developing world; in the next phase (2000–2016), it is likely that the middle and upper class workers have lost out. An appreciation of this effect can be gleaned from the following story.[6]

Mary and Sita: The sisters are not united

Here is the story of Mary and Sita, sisters united against a male-dominated civilization. But not by much else. Both were born in the 1960s. They were not only born in different countries but were also born in two different worlds—one in a lower middle class family in the richest country in the world, the US; and the other in a lower middle class family in the poorest country in the world (at that time), India. They had the same aspirations, and the same goals—to make the middle class dream come true.

When Mary and Sita were growing up, this is what they most likely witnessed, along with their counterparts in the rest of the world. During the twenty-year pre-globalization period (1960–1980), per capita income in India grew at 1.4 per cent per annum compared to the US growth rate of 2.3 per cent. During those days, an average person in a rich country (Mary), born in 1960, witnessed her parents' income increase by 63 per cent (till 1980). In contrast, an average person in a poor country (Sita) saw her parents' income increase by only 35 per cent, or almost *half* the rate of her US counterpart.

Mary went to college in 1978, and was able to *easily* enter the best universities. In sharp contrast, her own working period, however, has witnessed a glacial increase in family income. After thirty-five long years of hard work, such income is up only 50 per cent, and most of the increase is driven by the fact that she is now working along with her husband. In contrast, Sita's income is up nearly five-fold. To make matters worse, Mary finds that her children are finding great difficulty in entering the top universities, especially because of the large number of worthy applicants from Asia.

Put yourself in Mary's shoes—would you also not rant and rave against globalization? Of course, you would. But would you do so if you were Sita? Of course not, because you have never had it so good. She has become middle class, and it is her children (especially true for their counterpart Ms Chow from China) who are competing with Mary's kids at the best universities. It is more than likely that Ms Chow, daughter of a Tiger Mom,[7] is taking the position that Mary wanted for her daughter Linda. A decade later, maybe it will be Sita's granddaughter Divya who will snatch the college application away from Mary's granddaughter Susan. No matter how one slices the future, middle class America and the middle class West are witnessing disappointment.

China, mercantilism, and Trump

Two facts are immediately obvious about the period 1980–2010 (and continuing). First, that China, a very large economy, grew at miraculous rates for thirty continuous years. This rate of growth has never before been experienced by any country, and one can safely bet that this record will hold for generations to come. The second 'fact' is that China was able to gain an extra 1 to 3 per cent of GDP growth per annum, primarily because of mercantilism, a cause discussed at length in my book *Devaluing to Prosperity* (2012). This is what caused its miracle growth to be more pronounced than that of other East Asian economies like Japan, South Korea, and Taiwan.

Jobs have been lost in the West to competition from the East, primarily China. However, as emphasized by Edwards and Lawrence (2013), manufacturing jobs were being 'lost' in the US long before China entered the scene. In 1961, about 31 per cent of all jobs in the US were in manufacturing. By 1980, this share had shrunk to about 21 per cent. By 2010, this share was less than 10 per cent.

President Trump was elected in November 2016, and his campaign promise was to stop Chinese mercantilism. Ironically, and somewhat predictably, Trump's campaign promise of forcing the Chinese to revalue their currency, so that they have less competitive advantage and implicitly provide more Americans with jobs, has come a bit too late. The mercantilism game is over. It is not my argument that American jobs for Mary's daughter's cohort would have been aplenty if China had not exploited the system earlier. But it is my argument that the pace of job losses in the US (and the Western world in general) would have been slower had China *not* exploited via an undervalued currency.

In any case, the fact is that Trump's concern is a bit misguided. The same method and calculations which suggested that China had undervalued its currency between 1995 and 2010 now show that the yuan is very fairly valued and that China is no longer playing the beggar-thy-neighbour game. That is now a part of history—and perhaps why the American president has also been forced to retract.

But not all is good with globalization. There are losers, and in a reversal of history, the losers today are in the Western world. The arrival of this middle class, at lower wages, means a threat to competitors in the West. But the competitors in the West are those with higher wages, relative again to their internationally defined productivity. In the first instance of the evolution of the new globalization, i.e., in the 1990s and early 2000s, the most hurt community was that of the blue-collar workers, or workers in the bottom half, or two-thirds of the population. The anti-globalization protesters witnessed earlier most likely represented this losing class. The protests have now moved upscale, and today it is the Western middle class that is feeling the pain.

Brexit and Trump: Omens for Caesar?

In the classic play *Julius Caesar*, Shakespeare builds up the narrative to the inevitable assassination via a series of signals—or omens. Strange things begin to happen. Thunder and lightning, of course, but then macabre dreams, with blood flowing out of statues, owls shrieking at noon, heartless (literally) beasts, ghosts in the air (and in dreams), and soothsayers making accurate predictions—'Beware the Ides of March'. There are soothsayers today forecasting the end of globalization, or at least as we know it to be. They offer two omens of impending angst-filled doom: the vote by the British to exit from the European Union, and the election of Trump, against all odds, to win the 2016 Presidential election, and that too against a heretofore formidable female opponent Hillary Clinton. How valid are these omens?

Afghan immigrants voting for Brexit and Hillary losing to Trump

Most of us woke up to a surprise referendum result in June 2016—Britain, a land of globalization, a near equal financial capital of the world, the 'owner' of one of the most cosmopolitan cities, the country that once had the biggest Empire ever—yes, that same country was effectively, *de jure*, saying to the rest of the world—'We don't want you any more. You are not welcome on our shores any longer. And yes, soon start thinking about packing your bags, because we are British, *and* white.' The white part is critical in this politically correct world. But I exaggerate, of course I do. A week before the referendum, I happened to be in London and as is a political junkie's wont and custom, I did my 'survey' of which way the vote was going to go. The first cabbie was a twenty-nine-year-old Afghan, who had come to England ten years earlier. He was hesitant to talk, but he could recognize that I was from the same part of the world, i.e., we both should be against Brexit.

I persisted in my questioning—not which way he was going to vote (note to future junkies: that should always come last!) but which way he *thought* the vote was about to go. Exit, he said. And what about his vote? The same. I was shocked. A true-blooded brown immigrant, the one that the Brexit vote was loaded against, was voting Exit.

I persisted. Wouldn't you lose with Brexit? He didn't think he would lose, he was an immigrant, and believed that what Brexit would do is stop the other white immigrants (the Poles and the Romanians) from shirking work and taking welfare benefits that his taxes were paying for. For the record, no other cabbie had the same view as the Afghan—they were well-educated Uber drivers, some from professional jobs in the Middle East. And most were from the subcontinent.

What happened in 2016?

By now there are PhD theses being written on Brexit, but I did feel bad having missed this forecast. I was to feel worse five months later when I was certain (as I mentioned earlier, I have been a political-election junkie analyst and pollster for twenty-odd years—nay, a psephologist, a word Microsoft Word refuses to recognize but which simply means a pollster!) that Hillary Clinton was to win with a margin approaching double digits. That no pollster got the US election right—remember that all formal forecasts were made on the national vote and Clinton won that with a margin of 2.1 per cent, somewhat less than Obama's 3.9 per cent margin in 2012 but not that much less—was no consolation.

The opinion polls had Clinton winning easily against Trump,

and especially because it was believed (including by me) that women would favour her, and favour her by possibly a greater margin than they had favoured anyone in any other Presidential election. An additional reason for believing that Clinton would win by a comfortable margin was the fact that candidate Trump was believed to be a misogynist; so women, especially college-educated ones, were expected to vote *overwhelmingly* for her.

This did not happen; but what did happen was that Clinton obtained the highest number of votes from college graduates in post-war US elections—*and obtained the lowest share of votes from non-college graduates*. In the latter case, her vote share among non-college voters was 46 per cent, comparable to the previous low of 45 per cent obtained by Mondale against Reagan in 1984.

Clinton lost, but she obtained the same margin among college attendees as most Democrats in post-war history. In fact, more—in terms of a two-party contest, Hillary Clinton obtained 55 per cent of the college vote,[8] one of the highest in post-war US history, and more than even the 52 per cent obtained by Obama in 2012.

In a historical sense, neither middle America nor middle class America voted against Clinton. She did win the popular vote! College attendees (both college graduates and those who attended but did not graduate) now comprise 58 per cent of the voting age population in the US, compared to 42 per cent in 1984, and 24 per cent during Lyndon Johnson's clean sweep in 1964. In 2016, college graduates were 36 per cent of the labour force, compared to 22 per cent in 1964.

Close to two-thirds of Clinton's vote share was obtained from college graduates. As many have suspected, and rightly deduced, Clinton lost because of the overwhelming share of non-college voters who voted against her. Deploringly and tragically (and perhaps one of Shakespeare's omens), she had called non-college voters 'deplorables'.

Is the Trump victory portending the decline of globalization, world growth, and liberalism, as well as democracy? The point is simply that while we must draw lessons from Trump's victory, we should also appreciate the fact that the debate and the discussion would have been so different had Clinton managed to win just 80,000 extra votes in three states; close, very close, but no cigar.

Cesar Chavez and the Lettuce Revolt of the 1970s

It was the summer of 1976. I was a young, left-leaning, postdoctoral fellow at the Rand Corporation. Robert Topel (now a distinguished Professor of Economics at the University of Chicago) was an even younger (but not so left-leaning) predoctoral student at the University of California, Los Angeles (UCLA). Outside, sentiment was raging. For some years, Cesar Chavez (not to be confused with a Venezuelan despot with the same last name) had led a revolt for a fair minimum wage for the Mexican workers picking lettuce and grapes in California. I was naturally for Chavez's rebellion, and had stopped eating lettuce and grapes. Topel was (naturally?) against, and a quasi-heated argument ensued.

Mr Topel asked me—'So, you are concerned about poverty and the poor? Yes. But, as an economist, what would you say would happen to the employment of poor Mexican workers if wages were raised, *ceteris paribus*, of course?'[9]

'Well, at the margin, employment would go down,' I replied.

Topel continued, 'But what happens to the employment prospects and poverty levels of the Mexican worker coming to the US to seek better wages and eradicate penury and somewhat succeed in the pursuit of happiness?'

I got the point and haven't been left-leaning since. The point simply is this (as eloquently put by Paul Simon): One man's ceiling is another man's floor. Or an improvement in the wages of a Mexican worker in California may mean a decline in the living standards of a poorer Mexican in Mexico.

Globalization has been fair (and very good for the world)

John Rawls, possibly the most important 20th century political philosopher, had argued in his 1971 book *Theory of Justice* that a just moral position was best described as one which originated from a *veil of ignorance*. His thought experiment was as follows: assume you do not know what position (e.g., wealth) in society you will be born into, and you are asked to formulate policies for all of society; what policies will you advocate? The Rawlsian answer—the rational, just person will advocate the maximin policy, i.e., she will support that policy which maximizes the gains to the poorest, or equivalently, provide the maximum gains to those who have the minimum.

In Rawls' words, 'All social primary goods—liberty and opportunity, income and wealth, and the bases of self-respect—are to be distributed equally unless an unequal distribution of any or all of these goods is to the advantage of the least favored.'

That is exactly what globalization has done. No matter what the comparison—poor countries versus rich countries, the world as a whole, etc. (all detailed in Chapter 3, 4, etc.)—it is the case that the poorest have increased their incomes at a faster rate than the rich, and done so by an order of magnitude. For e.g., if the world is considered one country,[10] then the bottom 20 per cent increased their incomes by 193 per cent between 1980 and 2016, compared to a gain of only 71 per cent for the top 20 per cent. The top

1 per cent did a lot better than the top 20 per cent—their incomes increased by a healthy 86 per cent, but still well below the gains of the poorest.

These are per capita income gains in 2011 Purchasing Power Parity (PPP) prices.[11] The income gains in current income dollars are only possible for our complete set of 184 countries from 1994 onwards. Even with distorted exchange rates (induced by the large currency devaluations due to the Asian Financial Crisis [1997–1999], the poorest do significantly better than the rest. Between 2000–2016, *in US dollars*, the poorest 20 per cent witnessed a 176 per cent increase; the top 20 per cent enjoyed only a 59 per cent increase; and the top 1 per cent experienced an increase of 54 per cent (this after adjustment according to Piketty WID data).

Such data provides strong support for the notion that globalization has been very good for the poor, and especially the poorest. One can understand Mary's unhappiness; but how does one understand the view of a poor country intellectual who supports the rich, elitist anti-globalization movement? Perhaps these intellectuals have not really emerged from their feudal cocoon; perhaps they subliminally retain their colonial mentality. The leaders and operators of the anti-globalization movement are the formerly colonizing rich whites, who, as per their heritage, need non-white intellectuals as their disciples and followers. If the intellectuals were to argue for Mary's relative enrichment, they would be honest and would be constructive towards finding a better future for all, rich and poor.

Also, it is so much more righteous to fight 'in the name of the (non-white) poor'. But the price paid for such disingenuousness is that the bluff is easily called, and the intellectual barrenness easily exposed.

Understanding the political economy and the psychology of those opposed to globalization is important. There are several intermediate stages to how the world got to Brexit and Trump— and while some will continue to see a decline in their *relative* rate of improvement, news about the premature death of globalization is vastly exaggerated. As discussed in the concluding chapter, you can't fight Mother Nature, and education–globalization, warts and all, *is* globalization.

3

As the World Turns: From Colonialism to Freedom

Oh, and while the king was looking down
The jester stole his thorny crown
The courtroom was adjourned
No verdict was returned

—American Pie *by* Don McLean
(*music and lyrics by* Don McLean, American Pie, 1971)

It is an old, oft-repeated saying, but so true: the future and the present are best understood by understanding the past. If education is the wealth of the people, then a lack of education, or illiteracy, should mean lack of wealth, which translated means low incomes or poverty. That was the state of the world circa 1870; the average per capita income in the world was two-fifths of the level in the poorest region of the world today, Sub-Saharan Africa. Only 10 per cent of the world was literate then, and this was several decades after the Industrial Revolution. Incomes had been stagnant for hundreds of years. From complete stability at the zero level, per capita income growth in the Western countries finally crossed the 1 per cent per annum mark in 1870, and for some countries like the US and the UK, exceeded 1.5 per cent.

The world till 1950 was marked by colonialism and the lack of education in most parts. The US was a distinct outlier; the achievement of literacy in the US circa 1870 was larger than any other country.

But to what extent was globalization responsible for this shift, and how much did it benefit the poor? The truth is, not much at all. Economic historians have laboriously constructed estimates of incomes prior to the modern world (post-World War II and beginning 1950). Angus Maddison, belonging to the exclusive club of economists who *should* have got the Nobel Prize, constructed GDP data for a large set of countries, from 1500 to 2000. Such data is one of the major sources of information for economic historians.[12]

The next few pages summarize the data and the methodology operating behind the scenes to derive the conclusions of this book. Some readers may want to skip this short 'digression'. However, it is an absolutely important part of the analysis, and serves as an important go-to place if a reader wants to know how a particular number or conclusion was arrived at. We won't get into all the gory details (that will be too boring)—we'll just go with a succinct summary.

Regional income classification of countries: Setting up the data

Post-1950, the data used refers to the UN sponsored PPP data, where PPP stands for 'Purchasing Power Parity'. Given that US dollar exchange rates can be manipulated by policymakers and/or by the 'market', economists prefer the use of PPP values.[13]

Data: Regions

While we have a currency with which to evaluate outcomes (primarily PPP data post-1950[14] and Angus Maddison's 'equivalent' data prior to 1950), the construction of regions deserves a comment. Economists and international organizations divide the world into developed and developing. In the old days (circa 1960s), the developing world was composed of developing and the least developed. Today, the developing world is commonly subdivided into the relatively more developed (emerging markets) and developing. Political considerations also provide a division of Europe into Western Europe and Eastern Europe (the former Soviet Union). The Soviet Union is no more, and many Eastern European economies are just as developed as the Advanced Economies of the West, and are also now members of the European Union (though the UK has exited).

Obviously, all this is very confusing for an analyst surveying the last 300-odd years and projecting till 2030. Now if it's confusing for the analyst, no prizes for guessing that it's obviously triply confusing for the reader. For ease of analysis and communication and understanding, I propose a slight modification of the regions for this book. The West is Europe (including Russia and Eastern Europe), North America, Australia, and New Zealand. The rest of the world is sometimes referred to as the East, and sometimes as developing economies. West minus the former Soviet Union will be referred to as the Advanced Economies (AEs). The classification 'Rest' is used to refer to the world minus the AEs.

Separately, we have constructed the following five regions, a classification that helps in understanding the transformation of the world over the last fifty years, and should help in understanding the next twenty. The classification is part political and part economic. The first region is termed **US+** and consists of the US, Canada, Japan, Australia, New Zealand, and Israel. The second region is **Europe**, i.e., no distinction between East and West Europe or between belonging and not belonging to the European Union. Both Cyprus and Malta are considered part of Europe; they are classified in the grouping 'Middle East and North Africa' by the World Bank. The third grouping is just **China and India**, two countries that contain about two-fifths of the world's population. Region 4 is **AsiaX**, i.e., Asia excluding China and India, but including Turkey and Iran. The fifth region is the remainder of the economies consisting of Latin America, Middle East, and North Africa and Sub-Saharan Africa, and referred to as **LaMeSsa**.

Low incomes, little growth, and no education: Is there a link?

The reconstruction of the education profile, 1870 onwards, by Barro-Lee yields insights into the pattern of the level of incomes and education in the years preceding 1950.

Until 1820, world growth averaged only 0.04 per cent per annum, i.e., virtually no change in either absolute or relative living standards. The advent of the Industrial Revolution began to change the picture of stagnation and real per capita incomes in the West (US+ and Europe). Incomes grew at almost ten times the previous rate of 0.12 per cent per annum, and did so for the next 130 years. If it had not been for the interruption of the two world wars in the 20th century, this pace would have been a lot faster. There was almost zero growth for the remainder of the world for the long period between 1500 and 1820. The Industrial Revolution did help, but increased the growth rate to only 0.34 per cent per annum during the period 1820 to 1950.

Pattern of income distribution[15]

What one observes in 1950 is a world divided into two halves: the haves and have-nots; North and South; West and East; developed and developing, and now emerging. World inequality had zoomed to inconceivable heights in a space of just 150 years. Table 3.1 documents three statistics related to income inequality: the Gini, the share in incomes of the bottom 40 per cent (the traditional definition of the absolute poor), and the share of the top 1 per cent.

TABLE 3.1: WORLD INCOME INEQUALITY (1820–2030)

Year	Gini	Percentile Shares	
		Bottom 40	*Top 1*
1820	54.6	10.9	15.4
1850	58.4	9.3	16.4
1870	61.9	7.6	17.3
1913	66.8	5.2	19.1
1929	67.1	4.7	18.3
1938	67.1	4.6	17.2
1950	70.2	3.7	17.2

Source: Data from Piketty WID.world; World Economic Outlook, IMF (2017); author computations.

No matter what inequality statistic is looked at, the Industrial Revolution was not that good for *world* growth, and definitely not good for world inequality.

An easy definition of the Gini coefficient is as follows. If one person has all the income in an economy, then the Gini is a 100; if all individuals have the same income, then the Gini is zero. In 1820, the world Gini was at 54.6, with the top 1 per cent owning more than 15 per cent of total income; a century later (actually in 1913), the top 1 per cent owned 19.1 per cent of all income and the Gini had increased by 12 percentage points to 66.8.

Table 3.2 reports data for the five political-economic regions outlined above. No matter what the measure, US+ and Europe are similar, and the rest of the world different, and considerably poorer. There is no growth to speak of outside of US+ and Europe. Illiteracy was close to 100 per cent in populations outside of the West. This was the old divergence before the transformation.

TABLE 3.2: WORLD REGIONS: INCOME AND EDUCATION, 1700–1950

Variable–Time Period	US+	Europe	China–India	AsiaX	LaMeSsa	World
Income Growth (in % per year)						
1700–1820	0.21	0.11	-0.01	0.03	0.03	0.04
1820–1950	1.90	1.62	-0.59	0.70	0.02	0.62
Per Capita Income Levels (in 2011 PPP $)						
1870	1943	1911	589	677	677	1035
1950	10888	7265	507	1481	2968	3649
Illiteracy Rates (in %)						
1870	49.2	74.9	99.8	99.7	96.8	90.1
1950	2.2	11.8	70.9	69.9	63.6	49.5
Mean Years of Education						
1870	2.6	1.2	0.0	0.0	0.1	0.5
1950	8.1	5.2	1.5	1.5	1.9	3.1

Source: Penn World Table 6.1; Maddison (2006); World Economic Outlook, IMF (2017); Barro-Lee (2015).

Note: For the classification of countries according to regions, see text; AsiaX is Asia excluding India and China; LaMeSsa is Latin America, Middle East, and North Africa and Sub-Saharan Africa.

Why were the poor countries so poor?

There are alternative non-education explanations for the gap in incomes in the developing world before 1980 (and especially pre-1950), most importantly by Nobel laureate Arthur Lewis (1978), and by Williamson (2005, 2006). Chapter 2 of Lewis' *The Evolution of the International Economic Order* is titled 'The Division of the World'. He describes how the world, prior to the education expansion phase post-1950, was divided into several two halves: the have and have-nots, industry and agriculture, capital and labour. The developing countries had the raw materials, the now developed economies had the technology. Since industrialization was in full swing in the West, the developing countries got exciting prices for their raw materials and enjoyed a reasonable growth in incomes. The West industrialized.

Williamson has a parallel explanation to Lewis, and in its essence, similar.[16] He divides the world into the core (industrial, think West) and the periphery (primary producing, think non-West). The commodity boom of the late 19th century is also critical for him, for this boom allowed the terms of trade of the poor world to improve and their exports to surge. In his words: 'The secular rise in its terms of trade had powerful de-industrialization effects in the periphery which suppressed growth' (Williamson, 2005, abstract). Primary goods, demanded by the West, artificially and temporarily raised the prices of these goods significantly above fair value. This allowed incomes in the East to increase dramatically, and it is this increase in incomes which delayed industrialization (in the East).

For both Lewis and Williamson, there is also a commodity 'Dutch disease' aspect to the delayed industrialization story. The reference is to Tulipmania, the mother of all asset bubbles. The price of tulip bulbs (yes, tulip the flower) zoomed to astronomical levels in 1637 before crashing. At its peak, the price of one bulb was equal to ten times the annual wage of a skilled worker in Holland (hence, the Dutch disease).

As Clark (2005) documents, capital costs were similar across the world in the mid-19th century. For industrialization, wage differences mattered, and the commodity boom allowed the wages in the periphery to be much higher, and for much longer, than would have been dictated by 'deep' fundamentals. This was the tulip disease as the periphery priced itself out of competition for the production and export of manufactured goods.

Towards an alternative explanation for disparity in incomes

Though acknowledged after 1960, many economists are wary of looking at international developments of the 19th century through the lens of education. But recognition is accorded to education for demographic change; the reluctance is to provide primacy to education in the sphere of incomes and income growth. But let us look at the hints provided by the data on education. Figure 3.1 documents the spread of education during 1870–1950. *US+ and Europe had 70 per cent of the world's education in 1870, and 64 per cent of the world's income.* Just a coincidence the two shares match? No.

Colonization, education, and democracy

The 19th century was the age of colonization, and may contain some explanations as to why the poor countries did not progress— and most likely were not allowed to either. Nevertheless, the colonial episode provides one with a natural experiment—oh, how economists love natural experiments! As Africa began to be colonized, and colonial penetration into Asia increased, the colonial powers began to withdraw from Latin America. In 1804, Haiti became independent; between 1810 and 1824, several other countries were granted independence, for e.g., Mexico, Chile, and Colombia. By 1825, the job was complete as Bolivia was one of the last mainland colonies to become independent.[17] Around 1890, all of Latin America was independent, almost all of Africa and Asia colonized. The exceptions: in Africa, Ethiopia was never colonized; in Asia, China, Japan, and Thailand escaped the axe.

FIGURE 3.1: GLOBAL EDUCATION (1870-1950)—SHARES IN THE AVERAGE YEARS OF EDUCATION

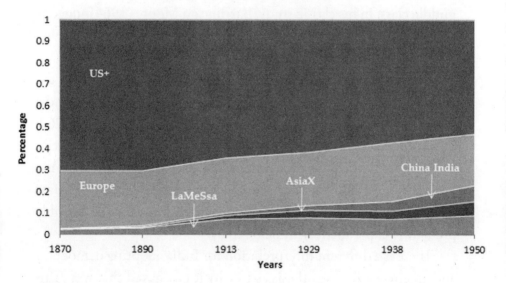

Source: Barro-Lee (2015).

Note: For classification of countries according to regions, see text; AsiaX is Asia excluding India and China; LaMeSsa is Latin America, Middle East, and North Africa and Sub-Saharan Africa.

The colonial period held a few positives for the developing countries ruled by Great Britain. At the time of India adopting a Constitution and a democratic form of government in 1950, only 25 per cent of the population was literate, and the average educational attainment of the adult population was one year. In 1870, estimates reveal that 75 per cent of the population in the US was literate. At the time of the Declaration of Independence in 1776, women and blacks were not educated, but amongst white males, the literacy rate was upwards of 50 per cent. No matter what the US education level was when it declared itself a democracy, the fact remains that education levels in India in 1950 were low, very low.

A strong, consistent correlate and cause for societies adopting a democratic form of government is a significant presence of the middle class. In his classic study, Barrington Moore (1964) suggests that the equation is 'no bourgeoisie, no democracy'. India in 1947 had almost no middle class.

Hence, one of the great political puzzles of history is the adoption and success of democracy in India. Very few gave India a chance to succeed as a democracy in 1947, or even in 1960; that it did may be more than just luck or foresight on the part of its founding fathers. It has been argued that it was because of the liberalism and humane nature of India's leaders, especially Prime Minister Jawaharlal Nehru, that India embarked upon its possibly premature experiment with democracy.

There is a different interpretation for India adopting democracy and an alternative hypothesis as to why it has stayed that way. This explanation, the one that provides a solution to Barrington Moore's puzzle, is that there is no puzzle. India adopted democracy because that was its 'heritage'. This 'inheritance' consisted of two aspects— India was both a British colony *and* it was ethnically and culturally diverse.

THE NEW WEALTH OF NATIONS

These two important factors contributed to India being and remaining a democracy, *despite* very low educational and middle class levels—as defined later and in *Second among Equals* (2007), less than 1 per cent of the population in India in 1950 could be thought of as belonging to the middle class. Certainly, India being a British colony turned out to be a very important determinant of democracy, at least in the early post-independence years, 1950–1970. The second reason, and one not conventionally discussed, is that the extremely heterogeneous nature of the Indian population, both conceptually and empirically, adds to the probability of the nation being democratic; this, for the obvious reason that only in a democracy do different and small ethnic groups have a say in governance; and being ethnically diverse means that there are several 'minority' groups wanting a say.

Evidence for this conclusion is provided by two sets of data. First, Table 3.3 shows the averages for British and non-British colonies for three different indicators of political freedom in 1970.[18] No matter what the index, British colonies obtain a higher value for 'democracy'.

TABLE 3.3: COLONIZATION AND POLITICAL FREEDOM

	Political Liberty	Executive Constraint	Democracy
	(1973)	(1960)	(1960)
British Colonies	3.2	3.5	2.8
Non-British Colonies	2.3	1.8	0.2

Source: Polity IV dataset.

Notes:
1. Political liberty index is from *Freedom in the World* (2017).[19]
2. Executive Constraint and Democracy indices are from Polity IV data.
3. For all indices, a higher value means greater political freedom.

The political freedom data suggests that at the time of independence there was a strong tendency in South Asia, ruled by the British, to lean towards a democracy. It may not be a coincidence that the four major South Asian economies (India, Pakistan, Bangladesh, Sri Lanka) all adopted democracy as their first form of government. They did not stay that way, most notably Pakistan. Some other factors may have played an important role in sustaining democracy in India.

In particular, ethnic diversity—as I have mentioned, the larger the diversity, the greater the probability of adopting a democratic form of government. It may not be a coincidence that the two ethnically diverse countries of South Asia—India and Sri Lanka—have persisted with democracy, and the two homogeneous societies—Bangladesh and Pakistan—have dabbled with both democracy and dictatorship.

Empirical analysis confirms the conclusion that both colonial heritage and ethnic diversity are important while explaining the presence of democracy in developing economies.[20] For 1960, the predicted probability for India being a democracy is a large 73 per cent (the highest probability was for South Africa at 76 per cent). Indeed, India has the fourth highest predicted probability. Both the world's richest democracy and the world's largest democracy were colonized by the British. In striking contrast, very few of the French (or German or Portuguese or Spanish) colonies have performed well on the democracy front, at least in the first few decades after independence.

Thus, India may have succeeded as a democracy because it was the *only* political system compatible with a heterogeneous population. Most analysts have focused on India's poverty and illiteracy in 1950 for not expecting India to be democratic, not fully appreciating that only a democracy can keep everyone the least unhappy. A democratic process gives, at least in theory, every group, and each individual a chance to participate in the decision-making. A small chance, one might say, but an infinitely higher chance than if the system was non-democratic—a monarchy or a communist set up, and all flavours in between. It is important to appreciate the existence of these small probabilities; the fact that they exist is the glue for solidifying expectations and for perpetuating democracy.

The logic of Indian democracy can therefore be summarized as follows.

The inheritance of British institutions meant a strong, positive initial proclivity towards democracy. The vote empowerment of different social, cultural, and religious groups meant that each group, especially the small groups, had a strong stake in democracy. A correlate of this empowerment was the desire among all groups for a united India, for only in a united India would each non-majority group have a voice. Hence, democracy was most likely the preferred choice among most sections of society.

4

Progress: Lost in 480 Years, Gained in 48 Years

Counting the cars
On the New Jersey Turnpike
They've all come
To look for America.

—America *by* Simon & Garfunkel
(*lyrics by* Paul Simon, Bookends, 1968)

The poor shall inherit the earth—or, to phrase it differently, how fast the world can change! Just forty years ago, both China and India were given up as basket cases (poor and without much chance of redemption); fifteen years from now, in PPP terms, the two largest economies in the world will be China and India. Only a few years ago, many were talking about deep poverty in India, and how the country had miles to go before it could begin to make a dent in its poverty, or make a significant contribution to world growth. Today, things have changed. China–India is the flavour of the year, and I'm reasonably certain also the flavour of the next few decades. One has to go deep into history to find another occasion when India and China were mentioned together with the same respect; indeed, one has to go back several thousand years. Not 'times-they-are-a'changin'' any more; times, they have changed.

It was not so long ago, in 1968 to be precise, that Gunnar Myrdal wrote his pessimistic Nobel Prize-winning treatise *Asian Drama: An Inquiry into the Poverty of Nations*. The book did not forecast a bright future for the Rest, especially for its populous Asian economies, China and India. Myrdal turned out to be quite wrong. However, that is not the point—we all make mistakes. The point is the extent to which the conventional, consensus opinion was out of sync with reality. Might it not also be the case that the same conventional, consensus opinion about the world being nasty today is wrong? If the growth rate for these two economies stays around its recent historical path, and even if the rest of the world accelerates its growth somewhat, then soon—predictably by 2028—history would have been repeated. The India–China share in world output (PPP terms) is projected to reach 35 per cent, or equal to their share of population in 2028—a phenomenon last seen more than 500 years ago. This is a good time to recall that just in 1980, the India–China world output share was less than 5 per cent.

Whether the time period is 1500 or 2016, the importance of India and China cannot be denied. When poor, they were important in that they were viewed as a burden to the rest of the world; with things improving in these two nations, their importance came to be perceived in terms of future potential; and when becoming largely middle class, both nations assumed significance as growth poles and magnets for the development of other emerging economies. Soon, their importance will lie in that they are *sources* of growth for the developed Western economies. In 2030, the average per capita income of India and China together is likely to be around $23,000 (China $29500 and India $16000, in 2011 PPP dollars); their joint population is likely to be close to 3 billion.[21] The entire developed world had the same level of per capita income—20,000 PPP dollars—just thirty-three years ago (in 1984). But their population was only about a fourth at 770 million.

As far back as 1700, average incomes and development in India and China were only about half the level of incomes in Great Britain—and the Industrial Revolution was yet to start in earnest. The recent past has been witness to the greatest of transformations: the eradication of absolute poverty for over a billion people. More than a third of the world's population was absolutely poor in 1980; less than a tenth of the world's population is absolutely poor today.

Equally important for the developing countries (again dominated by developments in China and India) has been the rapid expansion in schooling. In 1950, these economies had an average educational attainment of less than three years; in 1980, this average had increased to around five, and by 2016, the average had jumped to seven-and-a-half. By 2030, most parts of the developing world should be at ten years of schooling—a level where the developed world was at just thirty-five years ago. The story of the next thirty years is the near complete closing of this gap, with obvious (positive) implications for world inequality.

This book, as must now be evident, is about the course of prosperity over the last three hundred years, and the important role played by education in helping the poor countries move towards convergence with the rich countries. But the incomes in developing countries, especially China and India, were not always much below the world average. In 1500, the China–India average was close to the world average; two hundred years later, in 1700, the average was 10 per cent lower; in 1890, aided by the heavy presence of colonialism in India, the average became less than half.

In the good old days, between them, the two countries gave us the concept of zero, gave us the printing press, and China very likely discovered America in 1421, (some seventy years before the official belief that Christopher Columbus did it). And, of course, also provided the world with the new rage—the practice of yoga and/or the ability to stand on one's head. The importance of India and China, past, present, and future, is really about the importance of *size*. Size matters. Even when the two countries were very poor, absolutely and relative to any other group in the world, the gravity of their importance derived from the simple fact of size: they held 40 to 50 per cent of the world's population. If one now adds economic growth to this size, it becomes a gorilla of a story.

This is the story, consequently, of the world post-1980—with a rapid decline in world poverty and, for the first time, a rapid increase in developing country incomes, besides secular stagnation in Western economic growth (or stability at a low 1 to 2 per cent level).

In addition, the last twenty-odd years have also been the story of the unprecedented pace of growth in the size of the world's middle class. In the early years, until about 2000 or so, the world was known as Goldilocks country, but then the music stopped. While growth in developing countries continued to be strong, Western growth began to slow down and stagnate. For the East, however, growth has continued to be robust. Goldilocks still rules in close to 90 per cent of the world—and the opinion- and hashtag-makers are still in the developed world. The next twenty years will come to be known as the period when the world changes into a truly multipolar world—again, because of 'movements' in these two population giants.

China–India: From convergence to divergence

For centuries, India and China have been 'equal' in an extraordinary number of ways. Both have been large economies for hundreds of years; both were relatively rich until the Industrial Revolution began; both were absolutely poor until the events of the late 1940s. Both plummeted due to their separate, but equal, obsessions with planning and control during their dark aberrant decades between independence and the late 1970s. Both started economic reforms at almost exactly the same time, though China proceeded faster and quicker. China began serious economic reforms in 1978, India waited until 1991.

India's economic reforms were unquestionably later than

China's by these thirteen years, though there are some who believe that reforms actually had started in India as early as 1980. There is little question that the lag was significantly larger than the two years implied by 1978 (China) and 1980 (India). The price India has paid for gradualism in policy is that for a thousand years, its per capita income was within the range of 10 to 25 per cent of China's. This historical identity has radically changed.

Today, China's per capita income in PPP terms is more than twice that of India's. This glaring divergence is forgotten by most, especially when India–China comparisons are made. As far as infrastructure is concerned, India is a long way behind China (also expected, since China 'needed' infrastructure ten years earlier). But the comparison 'error' is understandable. After all, the world, and the two civilizations themselves, had always viewed India–China as equals. A mere thirty-five years of divergence is not even a ripple in history.

History has already begun to restore the old order, the old equivalence. A necessary condition for the China–India gap to be closed is for growth rates of India to exceed those of China. That has begun to happen, and will gather pace over the next decade. Indeed, the story of the world economy over the next twenty to thirty years will centre around how fast India is able to catch up with China. Today, India's per capita income is 44 per cent of China's; by 2030, relative income is expected to be at 53 per cent. That is how the catch-up accelerates. India today is best viewed as China with a five to fifteen year lag.

The entry of China and India into the world economy (largely China in the 1980s, with India joining in the early 1990s, and really making a mark around the turn of the 21st century) unleashed forces beyond most people's control and beyond anybody's imagination.

Today, there is a near identical role reversal. World growth is really about growth in the developing countries, the 'poor' world; it is growing much faster than the developed rich world, and its share in global output is no longer small. *Look no further than the East, young woman, look no further.*

Size does matter

It is alleged that, despite the alleged benefits of globalization, economic growth in developing countries (excluding China and India) is lower than in rich countries. In other words, world inequality has worsened. But excluding these two countries from the poorer countries is excluding half of the developing world's population; excluding these two countries is excluding 40 per cent of the world, which is frankly absurd.

For most questions, a simple analysis based on a large set of countries does yield the right answers. If fifty countries are rich, and 150 countries are poor, and if the rich countries all share something in common (X), and the poor countries also are similar but have something else in common (Y), then the search for the Holy Grail of explanations is nearly over—the rich are rich because of X, and the poor are poor because of Y. What gives weight to these arguments, and rightly so, is the evidence of the number of countries—the more the number of countries analyzed, the more convincing the evidence, and the more applicable the analysis.

In conventional terms, India and China are just two countries. But the size of these two nations is anything but conventional. A useful pointer is the fact that it takes the population of 171 countries to make one India, 174 countries to make one China.[22] So, an analysis of just two countries can be a useful summary of the experience of over 350 countries, i.e., the entire world twice over.

The country-level analysis of either India or China, or both, may be more useful than a cross-country analysis of 200 countries. Further, and most importantly, when inferences are drawn from an analysis of populations, then to exclude China and India is nothing short of a catastrophic mistake.

Cross-country studies can rightly be questioned on the grounds that different countries have different initial conditions, different cultures, different policies, and different nuances of development. How can common lessons be derived from such heterogeneity of experience? Advantage, India–China. The same intra-country culture, the same set of initial conditions, the same homogeneity *over time*, albeit considerable heterogeneity *at a point in time*. So while India and China are many countries, many cultures, many populations, their study may not be nearly as complex as studying the fortunes of a New Zealander versus the misfortunes of an Ethiopian.

The Great V: India and China, 1500–2030

For almost thousand years in history—between 1000 AD and 1980—India and China have been remarkably similar in economic terms, especially till 1950, with some important differences emerging between 1950 and 1980. They had the same per capita income, whether the time of measurement was the year 1000 or 1980; plus, they were the same geographical (obviously) and political union for most of this time period.[23] The divergence started to appear in 1980, and today, China is more than twice as 'rich' as India.

The thousand years of economic progress in India and China is summarized by the simple illustration in Figure 4.1. This figure reports the share of world population contained in India and China since 1500 AD and their share in world income. When the two shares are equal, it means that the average per capita income in India and China is equal to average world per capita income.

The figure conceals several mysteries. In the year 1500, India and China had almost 50 per cent share of the world's population and almost the same share of income. At that time, the two countries were about average and equal to one another. Not much mystery there.

Starting around 1600, the India–China share of world population started to increase, and peaked at 55 per cent in the early 19th century. The lag in the demographic transition among the Asian and African economies is well known, and well explained, so this increase in the India–China population share is not a secret. Developing countries had lower incomes, lower education, and higher fertility. By 1980, the share of population had declined to 38 per cent, but the share of world income reached a historical low of around 4.5 per cent for the 1970–80 decade.

What cries out for an explanation is this decline. The explanations for this Grand Canyon-like decline are, well, controversial. Hence, the emergence of the 'Why are countries poor?' or 'Why isn't the whole world developed?' industry. But since 1980, the two countries have seen a turnaround unlike any other in history (and possibly a phenomenon not to be witnessed in the future as well).

By 2016, India–China had increased their share of the world output to 25 per cent. And something monumental is literally just around the corner. In another thirteen years or so, if the *relative* growth rates of India and China are as they stand currently, as is most likely, then the global share of these two economies will be over 35 per cent—and equal to their share of the world population. Hence, India and China would have collectively recovered in forty-eight years what they had lost in 480 years. Now that's a revolution.

FIGURE 4.1: INDIA-CHINA: SHARE OF INCOME AND POPULATION IN THE WORLD (1500-2030)

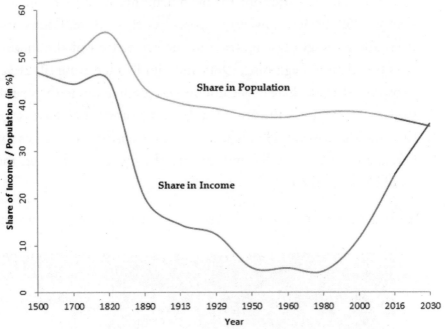

Source: Maddison (2006); Penn World Table 6.1; World Development Indicators, World Bank (2016); World Economic Outlook, IMF (2017); US Census Bureau (2016).

Note: Data for 2017-2022 has been obtained from IMF-WEO forecasts; 2023-2030 forecast is based on an extrapolation of the IMF-WEO data. All indicators 2017 onwards are extrapolations.

China-India, 1950-2030: An Overview

There is a link between the spread of education, especially college education, and the development and expansion of the middle class and incomes. The definition and estimation of the middle class is discussed in Chapter 10. How China and India are getting back their 'rightful' place in the world order is revealed in Figures 4.2 and 4.3. These charts illustrate the changes in different regions of the world from 1950 to 2030.

Middle Class: While Asia sees a marginal increase, Latin America and Sub-Saharan Africa don't show much improvement in income shares, 1950–2030. However, without much surprise, China and India show the greatest increase in the proportion of the middle class population, beginning 1980, and rapidly increasing till 2030, to own the largest share of the middle class population in the world. US+ and Europe, on the other hand, show a substantial decrease in their middle class populations; their losses transform into gains for China and India. In US+ and Europe, the movement is from the middle class to the rich.

FIGURE 4.2: SHARE OF THE MIDDLE CLASS IN THE WORLD (1950–2030)

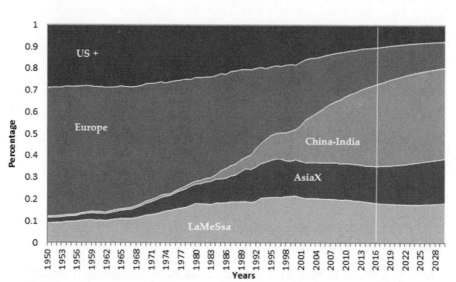

Source: Penn World Table 6.1; Maddison (2006); World Economic Outlook, IMF (2017); author computations.

Note: For the classification of countries according to regions, see text; AsiaX is Asia excluding India and China; LaMeSsa is Latin America, Middle East, and North Africa and Sub-Saharan Africa. All indicators 2017 onwards are extrapolations.

Income: Besides a staunch rise in middle class proportions, there is also a remarkable increase in the share of world income accruing to China and India, post-1980. Income shares decline for both US+ and Europe post the early 2000s; LaMeSsa and AsiaX hold on to their shares.

FIGURE 4.3: SHARE OF INCOME IN THE WORLD (1950-2030)

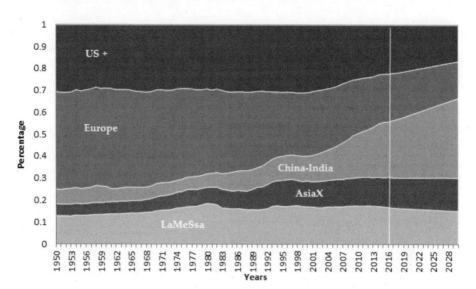

Source: Penn World Table 6.1; Maddison (2006); World Economic Outlook, IMF (2017); author computations.

Note: For the classification of countries according to regions, see text; AsiaX is Asia excluding India and China; LaMeSsa is Latin America, Middle East, and North Africa and Sub-Saharan Africa. All indicators 2017 onwards are extrapolations.

5

The Education–Income Connection

We don't need no education
We don't need no thought control
No dark sarcasm in the classroom
Teachers leave them kids alone

—Another Brick in the Wall *by* Pink Floyd
(*lyrics by* Roger Waters, The Wall, 1979)

There is a lot of talk about growing (sic) inequality of incomes. There is even greater talk about how the world is brutish and unequal, and how growing inequality in incomes is *the* scourge of our times. But there is very little serious talk about the equalizing force that is education. Instinctively, education is the most democratic of policy or parental interventions; once it is provided, no one knows where it can lead the recipient to, but, on average, the recipient does well!

Economists love the counter-factuals; if the question is what happens to Y when X exists, they like to derive the answer by reasoning, or imagining, Y *without* the presence of X. Let us do that with education. If your daughter didn't have any education, her life would be doomed; sure, she could live off inherited wealth, but then what would the daughter's daughter be able to achieve? One leading economist of the 20th century, Irving Fisher, talked about 'shirt sleeves to shirt sleeves in three generations', i.e., that inequality did not perpetuate itself and that, on an average, one came back to where one started in three generations (today three generations would be approximately a 100 years). In this instance of the progeny having zero education, it would be shirts to no shirts in one generation.

The example is a bit extreme, but no matter how much you tweak it, the answer remains the same—education helps one improve one's life's circumstances and increase possibilities. It is wealth that yields a flow of income, often an assured flow of income—which is why it should be called 'Not Fool's Gold'.

Let me give you one more example to explain the importance of education, before we proceed to analyze its effects. In a Rawlsian world, if there was only one game that your daughter could excel at, which one would you choose—football or cricket? The former involves literally no expenditure, a pair of legs and a round object that can be kicked. On the other hand, cricket (or baseball or tennis or golf) involves expenditure, and plenty of it. If you aren't rich, you aren't going to be able to play—even a non-Rawlsian individual would choose football for his progeny. And choose education, a cheap investment.

We view the *pursuit* of education as being instinctive, natural. We view this as being the natural order. It is today, but it wasn't always so. Indeed, one can trace this emphasis on education to the post-World War II period, and to be precise, to some mind-shattering work by Nobel Prize-winning economist Gary Becker. It was in the late 1950s that he made two propositions: that the amount of education (years of schooling) had a direct bearing on income, and that the decline in fertility was a direct consequence, a direct outcome, of the conscious trade-offs that parents made between the number of children that they would have, and the quality of life offered to their children. The quality was obtained by an investment in the schooling of the children. What parents desired was not children but child services; and child services could be estimated from the simple multiplication of the quantity and quality (education years) of children.

This 'simple' formulation helped explain several phenomena. Why did the rich have fewer kids? Because they wanted to educate their kids better. Why did the poor have more kids? Because they could not afford schooling for their children and/or the schools were not there.

The US realized this simple proposition before the rest of the world—and before the leader of the Industrial Revolution, Great Britain. In 1870, 22 per cent of the population had obtained primary education in Great Britain; the comparable number for the US—58 per cent.[24] Evidently, the UK was richer by about 25 per cent. It was the world's largest and most successful colonizer, but shockingly close to 80 per cent of its population had no schooling in the 19th century. In contrast, in its former colony, the US, illiteracy had dropped to a mere 25 per cent.

The effects of Britain, and other countries, not recognizing the fundamental role of education in transforming societies and accelerating growth was soon made obvious. By 1913, illiteracy in the US had dropped to less than 5 per cent, while in Britain it was still a quarter (Table 5.1). The average school education attainment in the US was close to seven years, while in Britain, it was less than four. And the US was now the richest country in the world, with per capita incomes close to 6000, in comparison to Britain, whose per capita income was lagging behind at 5300 (in 1996 PPP $).

TABLE 5.1: EDUCATION AND INCOME (1850-1913)

Country	Year			
	1850	*1870*	*1890*	*1913*
Illiterates (in %)				
United States		25.2	8.4	4.7
Sweden		21.7	15.1	8.8
United Kingdom		78.0	58.8	23.2
Japan		80.5	55.5	26.2

Country	Year			
	1850	*1870*	*1890*	*1913*
China		100.0	99.9	98.9
India		99.6	98.2	90.7
Primary Enrolment Ratio				
United States	80.1	100	100	100
Sweden	89.4	100	100	100
United Kingdom	24.1	39.0	93.1	100
Japan	22.6	41.4	86.8	96.6
China	0.0	0.1	0.6	4.3
India	0.4	1.5	6.1	10.1
Attended Primary School (in %)				
United States		57.9	65.4	51.4
Sweden		72.0	76.8	83.3
United Kingdom		21.7	40.2	69.6
Japan		19.5	44.4	70.0
China		0.0	0.1	1.0
India		0.1	1.2	8.0
Mean Years of Education				
United States		4.3	5.6	6.9
Sweden		3.6	4.1	4.6
United Kingdom		0.9	1.8	3.9
Japan		0.5	1.3	2.8
China		0.0	0.0	0.0
India		0.0	0.1	0.4
Annual Per Capita Income (1996 PPP $)				
United States		2738	3796	5950
Sweden		1862	2336	3468
United Kingdom		3468	4344	5329

Country	Year			
	1850	1870	1890	1913
Japan		840	1168	1606
China		584	584	584
India		621	657	767

Source: Barro-Lee (2015) for education data; author's calculations.

It is likely that some part of the explanation for the higher levels of literacy observed in the US was due to its open door immigration policy. The land of opportunity beckoned early white settlers. Predictably, the poorest and the less-educated could not afford the journey. Hence, it wasn't just educational policy that yielded higher educational attainment in the US, but also a more enlightened immigration policy. While there may be some truth to this speculation and assertion, school enrolment data does suggest that the US was well ahead of its peers.[25]

In any case, Britain's 'bad' elitist policy towards education rubbed off on the leaders of its colonies. Jawaharlal Nehru, himself an erudite liberal educated at Oxford, felt the country had to build temples of excellence (read universities), *before* expanding primary and secondary education. This policy, in retrospect (and prospect), was elitist, and India paid for it through the perpetuation of large absolute poverty for a lot longer, and growth rates a lot slower, than in the counterfactual of expanding primary and secondary schooling. India did not learn the lesson from its master—the bigger surprise is that the master (England) did not learn the lesson from its own former-student, the US. But we are digressing.

Let us first get back to Becker discovering home truths. Both rich and poor parents desire the same amount of child services. A simple extension of the quantity–quality formulation was that the rich were more likely to send their kids to private schools, and the rich kids were more likely to go to college (more quality in the form of more years of schooling). The rich would also, on an average, have fewer kids.

All of this is obvious, you say. And you are right. As I have always believed, genius is something that is obvious *ex post*. The great fertility transition in Europe had happened more than a hundred years before Becker's elegant formulation, and economists and sociologists have explained it, in part, as the result of the quantity–quality tradeoff.

I was lucky to have parents who instinctively understood the value of education. I was sent to Purdue University for my undergraduate studies in January 1965, and financed by my emerging middle class[26] parents who believed that education, and especially a foreign education, was the path to riches and success. At that time, the rich and savvy children of even savvier (and richer) parents, sent their children to the University of Oxford or the University of Cambridge—and if that did not work, then the London School of Economics (LSE) was their next preference. A US education was just beginning to be recognized as better than the rest of the world in terms of quality and experience, and Purdue, my alma mater, was a very good school for engineering, but nowhere in the top league for the liberal arts. And the trend towards more and more students opting for engineering had just begun, so I guess I was part of at least one set of pioneers.

The point I wish to make is that the formalization of thinking about education and income—the education–income connection—was first made by Becker. And it wasn't until the late 1960s that explicit linkages between education and income began to be explored. In one of my earliest courses in economics and the application of statistics to the study of economics (aka econometrics), Orley Ashenfelter had discussed a recently published research paper from one of the leading economics journals, *American Economic Review*. This paper (Hause, 1971) had one of the best titles—'If You Are So Smart, Why Aren't You Rich'—and related the income of an individual to his education. (Remember, this was in the early 1970s and the usage of 'her' had yet to be invented, but was about to be conceived.)

In the Hause paper, one of the few factors that explained income was education. However, the total variation in earnings explained by 'Human Capital Models' was around 10 per cent, often less. The variation explained by the model is what economists call R^2—a value which indicates the tightness in the overall relationship between all the determinants and the variable one is trying to explain (the dependent variable). Let us dwell a bit on the 10 per cent; what was empirically asserted is that human capital in the 1960s only explained 10 per cent of the total variation in earnings. In other words, several other factors cause differences in earnings across individuals—sex, occupation, physical assets like land, financial assets, and perhaps most importantly, unmeasured ability. Determinants like age and experience are an integral part of the human capital model.

What we know for a fact, low statistical explanation and all, is that our understanding of what is the major determinant of individual income—and by extension the determinant of income distribution in the world—was based on this seemingly fragile result. As history was to prove (and that is what this book is based on), this result was one of the most important empirical findings of the 20th century. Embedded in the human capital and income relationship being estimated post-Becker is the statistical significance of years of schooling in explaining income. Different from an R^2 but similar is the t-statistic of a variable in an estimated economic model. The t-statistic measures the tightness of the relationship between an individual determinant and the variable being explained.[27]

The t-statistic for years of schooling was very high, suggesting a close connection between education (years of schooling) and income (or wages).[28] It is this tightness that caused hundreds of studies to sail forth into a PhD; today, there are no more empirical studies being conducted on whether education is the most important determinant of an individual's income. However, and this is a most unfortunate neglect, there are very few studies documenting the wealth embodied in education.[29] How serious this omission is can be derived from the fact that for over 95 per cent of the individuals in the world, education is not *a* source of wealth, but *the* source of wealth. The significance of this neglect is further documented in Chapter 6 (spoiler alert: education wealth is extremely important in estimating the total wealth of individuals).

Let me tell you the rest of the Ashtenfelter–Hause story. I remember that class distinctly. My good friend Orley's classes were distinguished by content and humour.[30] But in this instance, I inadvertently provided some ground for mirth. One of the explanatory factors for income, in addition to years of schooling, in the Hause paper discussed by Ashenfelter was a Jewish dummy. For the uninitiated, in regression analysis, one often puts in a catch-all (0,1) variable—in this instance, whether the person whose earnings was being explained was Jewish (dummy on and equal to 1) or not (dummy off and equal to 0). The Jewish dummy was very statistically significant and had a coefficient of around 0.1, i.e., being Jewish meant that one's earnings were 10 per cent higher than that of a non-Jewish person with identical attributes. I raised my hand and asked, 'Sir (being an Indian, you never addressed professors by name), if I converted to Judaism would my earnings be 10 per cent higher?' I forget Ashenfelter's response but I did get credit for being witty.

I was to pursue the Jewish dummy in some detail a few years later. And it was my very good friend Robert Lawrence (also Jewish, and now a Professor at Harvard), who explained that in order to be both 'good' and Jewish, one had to be able to read the holy book, the Torah. This simple requirement explains a lot about the pursuit of education amongst those born as Jews. Regarding the extra human capital among those born Jewish, there are many asides by economists, including one verified by history: 'The reason Jews invested so much in education was because this was the only asset they could flee with when they faced persecution.'

In stark contrast to the requirement of reading the Torah by the high priests of Judaism, the high priests of India, the Brahmins, ensured that no one besides them would be able to read *any* of the many holy books that constitute Hinduism.

But education–globalization and a Mother Nature induced demand for education have reduced the influence of traditional religion. Thank God, did you say!

6

Education As Wealth

I can see clearly now the rain is gone
I can see all obstacles in my way
Gone are the dark clouds that had me blind
It's gonna be a bright (bright)
bright (bright) sunshiny day

—I Can See Clearly Now *by* Jimmy Cliff, 1993
(*original performance and lyrics by* Johnny Nash, 1972)

As mentioned in the previous chapter, there are, literally, hundreds of studies across the world (possibly thousands) which document the close connection between education and income. There are also countless studies on the different rates of return to different levels of schooling. Investment in education is well recognized as the major or primary investment for most families in the world. This investment is in an asset, and one that yields a constant flow of income, i.e., *acquisition of education is acquisition of wealth*. Yet, despite its importance and the constant outpourings of despair in the media about severe wealth inequality in the world, there are not many studies which estimate the wealth contained in educational attainment. Indeed, there isn't a single study that provides estimates of education wealth for different countries and different years.

We attempt to remedy this shortcoming. But first, some commentary on the data that presently does exist on the distribution of conventionally defined wealth in the world.

The literature we have paints some horrific stories. As is expected in this US-centric discussion, the painting first starts with the unequal nature of income growth in the US. It is noted that income growth in the US has been very uneven for the last thirty years. The top 1 per cent in the US had over 22 per cent of the total income in 2015, which is nearly double the 13 per cent share they had just thirty years ago.

The most recent Oxfam Report of January 2017 was titled 'An Economy for the 99%' with the subtitle: 'It's time to build a human economy that benefits everyone, not just the privileged few'. NGOs have an uncanny touch, and they generally, and accurately, reflect the mood of the people. But they are not always so accurate about the facts as we will soon see. The following paragraph from the report is noteworthy:

> It is four years since the World Economic Forum identified rising economic inequality as a major threat to social stability, and three years since the World Bank twinned its goal for ending poverty with the need for shared prosperity. Since then, and despite world leaders signing up to a global goal to reduce inequality, the gap between the rich and the rest has widened. This cannot continue. As President Obama told the UN General Assembly in his departing speech in September 2016: 'A world where 1% of humanity controls as much wealth as the bottom 99% will never be stable.'

Note that here the control of the top 1 per cent refers to wealth, not income. Notice also how seamlessly the report goes from widening economic inequality in the US to widening inequality in the world—and, of course, with equal facility, to world wealth inequality, as asserted by Credit Suisse in their now popular annual reproduction of world wealth inequality and the scary and disturbing reality of the increasing number of billionaires in the world, especially in the poor developing countries.

Before we go ahead, let's discuss the analytical base of Oxfam's conclusions a bit more. Oxfam boldly continues expressing its worries as below, digging itself deeper into a hole. (I have inserted numbers to this worry list for reference below.)

1. Yet the global inequality crisis continues unabated.
2. Since 2015, the richest 1% has owned more wealth than the rest of the planet.
3. The incomes of the poorest 10% of people increased by less than $3 a year between 1988 and 2011, while the incomes of the richest 1% increased 182 times as much [for the US].
4. In the US, new research by economist Thomas Piketty shows that over the last 30 years the growth in the incomes of the bottom 50% has been zero, whereas incomes of the top 1% have grown 300%.
5. Left unchecked, growing inequality threatens to pull our societies apart. It increases crime and insecurity, and undermines the fight to end poverty. It leaves more people living in fear and fewer in hope.

This is a lot of 'information', and even more despair. However, before jumping to any conclusions, examining the context of these warnings and their veracity is worthwhile. Oxfam is not alone in reaching these conclusions. As the report quotes President Obama, it is presumed that some very senior economists in the US have vetted the conclusions, and given it their 'Good Housekeeping' seal. Let us first examine the conclusions pertaining to income distribution.

It is important to recognize, at the outset, that any discussion about the twin emotive issues of poverty and inequality is laced with not just ideology, but deep ideology. And no one is immune from this 'bias', not me, not you, not Marx, not Reagan, not Amartya Sen, and definitely not Oxfam—indeed, no one. This is a cross that all analysts have to bear.

It is impossible to live in argumentative India and not be faced, daily, with this ideological bias. I want to emphasize that I also suffer from such a bias. At the same time, I, like many others, want to filter out ideology to the extent possible and arrive at a set of facts first. And only then, if need be, embellish it later with ideology.

Table 6.1 below assembles data from official sources; income distribution in the US is forced to take the same shape—especially for the top 10, 5, and 1 per cent—as contained in the WID.world database.

TABLE 6.1: FEAR MONGERING ABOUT INEQUALITY—US, 1985 AND 2015

Variables	Year		Per Cent Change
	1985	*2015*	
GDP *(in current $, billion)*	4.4	18.0	313.8
Share of top 1% in total income	12.7	22.0	
(in '000)			
GDP per capital *(current $)*	18.1	55.5	206.5
Real GDP per capita (2011 prices)	32.7	52.1	59.4
Real per capita income (Households)	28.9	44.7	54.7
Mean income of bottom 50%	10.9	13.5	23.4
Mean income of top 1%	346.8	985.1	184.1

Source: Data from Piketty's WID.world; World Economic Outlook, IMF (2017); author computations.

The Oxfam assertions don't seem right even from a cursory glance. Incomes of the bottom 50 per cent increased by 23 per cent, not 0 per cent. The top 1 per cent increased their share from 12.7 per cent to 22 per cent, but their mean incomes did not increase by 300 per cent. Rather that increase was considerably less at 184 per cent. So where does the 300 per cent figure come from? Maybe from the increase in nominal GDP.

The 'fact' that the bottom 10 per cent has witnessed an increase of income of less than US $3 a year between 1988 and 2011 is worrying in itself. This is one figure that the Oxfam report gets correct. But make note that the 'less than $3' increase actually represents a 23 per cent increase for the bottom 50 per cent between 1985 and 2015. The bottom 99 per cent increased their incomes by 37 per cent. So it is like the whole class failed, except one person (the top 1 per cent), i.e., 99 per cent of the population had near equal (and low) annual rates of growth, and the top 1 per cent had a high rate of growth (they passed the exam!).

Oxfam worry numbers 1 and 5 are discussed in detail in the next few chapters, but let us turn to the seemingly factual statistic in the Oxfam list—that the top 1 per cent owns more wealth than the rest of the planet. This is a statistic from the latest Credit Suisse report on the subject, so we cannot blame Oxfam.

The Credit Suisse report seems accurate for what it purports to collect—data on land and financial wealth in the world, and who owns it. I have no problem with their estimates or methods of calculation. But I do have a problem, a rather big problem, with those who ignore the major form of wealth of the bottom 99 per cent—the wealth embedded in their education.

What is income? A flow of money from an asset. What is an asset? Wealth is. Anything that yields a flow of income is wealth. Therefore, land or a house is an asset because it yields a flow of income. Cows that give you milk are wealth (some Hindus consider the cow an asset superior to all other forms of wealth). Why have parents invested in their children's education? Precisely for the same reason, because it is an asset. It is actually a double form of wealth— education increases the utility of the children for the parents (you can have better conversations, just ask Tiger Moms) *and* provides an income flow to their children. Given its importance, why has there not been any estimate of this wealth, for the bottom 99 per cent as well as the top 1 per cent? The answer to this could be because the numbers may reveal an uncomfortable reality. It's a possibility, but we don't know the numbers, yet. A preliminary estimate of the wealth distribution contained in education is the primary purpose of this chapter.

But before going there, let's take another detour towards estimating the wealth in education.

Estimating the wealth in education

There is data on years of schooling and rates of return to schooling. A conservative estimate of the rate of return to education is that it is the same for all years of schooling at around 10 per cent. However, there is a problem—the quality of schooling varies significantly between countries. Simply put, an average Princeton graduate has a higher quality of education than an average student at an average US university, and somewhat higher than those graduating from the best universities in India, China, or most universities in the developing world. The quality of the university one graduates from has some bearing on one's lifetime earnings; there will be differences and surprises, of course, but we are talking of averages here. One would think that it is a near impossible task to adjust college attendance data for school quality and/or productivity of workers residing in different countries—it's a difficult exercise, yes, but not impossible.

Indeed, the PPP data we had talked about in an earlier chapter can be used to adjust for productivity differences, and/or wage differences. A personal example of mine will help substantiate this. I returned to India in 1996 after both education and work experience in the US. My wage, when converted into US dollars, dropped to (approximately) a quarter of what I was earning in the US. I received a US college education, so that was not a factor in my receiving a lower wage in India. I was doing the same work as in the US, and delivering the same output, so there was no possibility of my productivity being lower. So why the lower wage then, and that too by such a large magnitude?

Let us look at the PPP data for India for the year 1996. The exchange rate with respect to the US dollar was Rs 36; the PPP exchange rate was Rs 9 to 1 PPP $. *This implies that 1 US dollar bought the same amount of goods and services in India as 25 PPP cents.* Stated differently, but equivalently, my earnings in PPP $ were four times the earnings in US$; hence, my one-fourth earnings in US dollars was identical to my purchasing power in the US. This is what the market is supposed to do—equalize wages to productivity. In my case, while I was getting a lower wage in US dollars, I was receiving the same PPP wage as I did in the US (1 PPP $ = 1 US $ in the US).

The bottom line is that there is a lot of information contained in PPP exchange rates and dollar exchange rates. This information is exploited in estimating the supply of skilled labour in different countries. In 2016, 1 US dollar was equal to 26 PPP cents in India (coincidentally, almost the same as in 1996) and 53 PPP cents in China. Thus, the number of 'effective' Chinese college graduates in 2016 would be 0.53 times the actual number of graduates; in India, the adjustment factor would be 0.26.[31] In this manner, years of schooling across different countries (and time) can be converted into adjusted (read: comparable) years of schooling.

Educational wealth in the world

How much is the wealth embedded in education in 2016? The answer is very revealing—it is higher than financial wealth. That this should be expected is provided by the following heuristic explanation. World GDP in 2016, in US dollars, was 75 trillion. For most countries, the share of labour in total GDP is about 40 to 50 per cent. Taking the lower 40 per cent level as representative of income accruing to labour via education, US $30 trillion can be considered as the flow of income emerging from the asset (wealth) owned by labour. This is a flow forever; the simple formula for converting a perpetual flow into a stock (wealth) is the division of the flow by the applicable interest rate. Even if a high rate of interest is assumed, say 7.5 per cent, one obtains that education wealth in 2016 was equal to US $400 trillion.[32]

The Barro-Lee data yields the average years of schooling for each country and year. This data is transformed into 'equivalent' dollars of wealth for all countries and years. Note that the distribution of education wealth is more equal than the distribution of financial wealth. This *has* to be the case because education is more equally distributed than income.

Like football, education is the most democratic of policy interventions, and achievements. This is because human capital has both a natural floor and a natural ceiling. The floor is zero (illiterate labour with zero education wealth) and the ceiling is sixteen to twenty years (for medicine). But not everybody goes on to become a doctor or obtain a PhD (i.e., average years of schooling close to twenty-plus). It is noteworthy that in the US, the country with the largest number of college graduates, the average years of education of the population is 'only' thirteen-and-a-half, and this is slated to rise to fourteen over the next fifteen years.

If the whole world was at zero years of education (as in the year 1700 and before) the world would have zero education wealth inequality. With the expansion of education, the world is becoming more equal. In 1870, the Gini for years of schooling was as high as 91, i.e., very few people had education. In 1950, this inequality had declined to 66.8, and by 2016, the Gini for years of schooling was at a benign 32.9.

Towards estimating the wealth in education

There are various steps involved in estimating the wealth embodied in education, and are detailed in Bhalla (2017a). The simple idea is to obtain the distribution of wage earnings according to the various stages of education for which we have the Barro-Lee data. There are seven such stages: illiterate, primary school attended, primary school completed, and the same for secondary and tertiary education. The illiterates are attributed a 'basic income' flow based on the fraction of illiterates in the population; for countries with less than 5 per cent illiteracy, the mean income of the bottom 5 per cent of the population is taken as representative. Once the base income is obtained, then the total income from years of education is estimated on the basis of a 10 per cent rate of return for each year of education.

Two further adjustments are needed. First, an adjustment for schooling quality. Financial wealth is based on 'market' values of assets. The market value of education is the market wage (income) in PPP terms; hence, variation in schooling quality is proxied by the level of the real exchange rate.[33] Some representative values for 2016: all advanced economies at 1 (same quality of education), Brazil at 0.57, China at 0.52, India at 0.26 and South Korea at 0.73. The income flow from education is adjusted by these factors.

81

For example, the PPP income originating from twelve years of education in South Korea is multiplied by 0.73; in recent years, the adjustment factor for AEs is close to unity.

What the above exercise yields is the flow of income from education. To convert the flow into wealth, one needs an interest rate, i.e., the rate of interest on borrowings for the pursuit of education. This is conservatively taken to be a high 7.5 per cent. On the basis of this high discount rate, a conservative (minimum) estimate of the wealth of education in the world in 2016 is estimated to be US $330 trillion.

Financial wealth is estimated by Credit Suisse to be US $256 trillion in 2016 and US $111 trillion in the year 2000. For 2000, our estimate of education wealth in the world is US $185 trillion.

Table 6.2 presents data for a few countries on education wealth for the year 2016. Some preliminary conclusions: the Gini for education wealth is estimated to be 76, the same as in 2011. The Gini for financial wealth (Credit Suisse) for 2011 is reported to be 89.3; unfortunately, the Credit Suisse Gini for 2016 has not been reported.

The more interesting comparison with financial wealth data is with the share of the top 1 per cent; for financial wealth it is more than 50 per cent; for education wealth, the share of the top 1 per cent is in the high teens.

Incorporation of education wealth data into total wealth (as it should be) provides a very different perspective on wealth distribution. Because of the highly unequal nature of financial wealth, and the relatively equal level of education wealth, the share of the top 1 per cent in total wealth is close to 31 per cent, still relatively unequal but not as unequal as owning more than 50 per cent.

TABLE 6.2: EDUCATION WEALTH, SELECT COUNTRIES (2016)

Countries	Education Wealth	Share of the Top 1%	Gini
	(in trillions)	(in per cent)	(in per cent)
Advanced Economies			
Germany	17.4	8.5	43.1
UK	11.8	8.5	46.0
US	81.0	10.4	51.6
Developing Economies			
Brazil	9.0	16.7	57.1
Chile	1.3	19.0	54.4
China	56.8	11.9	63.4
India	6.9	19.2	63.3
Indonesia	4.0	12.1	49.6
Iran	1.3	15.2	53.7
South Korea	6.4	4.7	33.9
Turkey	2.8	19.0	59.7
World	330	17.7	76.0

Source: Barro-Lee (2015); author computations.

Inequalities: Schooling, income, and education wealth

The changing pattern of world inequality is documented in Figure 6.1. It reports on three inequalities, namely, income, wealth, and years of schooling (adjusted for quality of schooling). The broad trends are as follows:

Income Inequality: In 1890, the income Gini was at 61.4, and after reaching a peak of 70.7 in 1973, it has now declined to the level last obtained in 1890. What is playing a large part in the decline in income inequality is the decline in education inequality.

Education Inequality: In 1870, educational attainment was highly unequal, with a Gini level of 91.3.[34] There is no recorded income Gini which is this high. In 2000, education had become somewhat equal, with a Gini of 58. In 2016, the constantly declining education Gini had reached 45.8, and is slated to gradually decline to around 43 by 2030. Not shown in the figure is the 'pure' education Gini, i.e., education inequality entirely based on years of schooling, regardless of quality. This Gini in 2016 was a relatively equal 32.9, and is expected to decrease further and reach 29 by 2030. Some perspective on this equality is provided by noting the share of the top 1 per cent in years of schooling in 2016—merely 2.1 per cent.

Education Wealth Inequality: The pattern of education wealth Gini closely follows that of the education (years of schooling) Gini. Similar to education inequality, the education wealth (hereafter e-wealth) has been adjusted for education quality (same as conversions of dollar income to PPP $ incomes). It is interesting to note that even though e-wealth and years of schooling saw a consistent decline in inequality since 1870, income inequality increased till about 2000. Post-2000, both income and e-wealth Gini have exhibited the same trend as education years Gini. This further reaffirms our notion—education is the driving force of equality.

Figure 6.1 captures the changing, and changed, world very succinctly—the forces at work are unstoppable. World education, and hence, world income, inequality is destined to levels last seen 150 years ago, and in the case of income, we are at nearly the level of 1890. Education to the people is (economic) power to the people.

FIGURE 6.1: INEQUALITY (GINI) IN INCOME, WEALTH, AND SCHOOLING

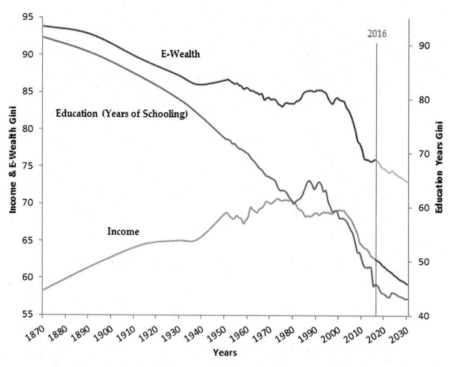

Source: Barro-Lee (2015); Piketty WID.world; Inequality measured on the basis of average years of schooling.

Note: Education wealth (E-Wealth) is measured as schooling years adjusted by the PPP exchange rate (see text). All indicators 2017 onwards are extrapolations.

7

Unlimited Supply of Skilled Labour (USSL): Causes and Consequences

Once upon a time there was a tavern
Where we used to raise a glass or two
Remember how we laughed away the hours
And dreamed of all the great things we could do
Those were the days my friend
We thought they'd never end

—Those were the Days *by* Mary Hopkin
(*lyrics by* Boris Fomin & Gene Raskin, Single, 1968)

E ducation improves one's own welfare and wealth. But it has ramifications far beyond individual borders, and will continue to as long as the world has trade. In the period between the 1960s and 1980s, news media and policymaking were all about developments in economies outside of the prosperous Western world, i.e., the talk and thinking, and all discussions to do with poverty were about the *other* 81 per cent of the world's population. Today, that *other* holds about 87 per cent of the world's population.

Interestingly, now, the attention, concern, angst, and hype are almost all about complications in the West. There are three central problems that are of major concern now, and have been for at least the past couple of decades. There is the problem of secular stagnation in economic growth in the Western world; low GDP growth; and the associated low growth in real wages. There is concern over growing inequality among advanced industrial economies. And there is the puzzle of low inflation in the developed world. If you have noted that all three refer to the same set of countries, then you are absolutely right. Even partial exposure to any form of the media (and no one is living in a cave or under a rock any more) would convince anyone that the entire world is suffering from all the above three 'Big Picture' macroeconomic trends.

We have been at pains to outline, throughout this book, that generalizations for the world do not follow from generalizations about the West. They never did, and the linkage is weak today as well. However, there is one development that helps explain the three 'problems' noted above—it is the expansion of college education in the Rest of the world over the last fifty years (Rest defined as the world minus the Advanced Economies [AEs]).

This expansion limits the real wage increase of college workers in the US—this is the much talked about secular stagnation. It allows real wages in the Rest to expand at a faster pace than the West, and hence leads to a decline in world income inequality. Finally, it indirectly *can* lead to low inflation in the West, and low inflation globally. We address each of these relationships below.

The evolution of real wages in the West: A case study of the US

The US labour market is one of the most studied markets in the world. Over the last thirty years, the real hourly wages of workers with high school qualifications or lower levels of education have been constant or declining. For example, the hourly wage of a worker with less than a high school education was around $15.5 an hour circa 1980 (in 2016 prices); in 2016, this wage had declined to $13.2. For a high school graduate, the wage has stayed constant at $17.2; for a person with some college attendance, but not a degree, the wage has increased marginally from $18.6 to $19.1. In 1980, 81 per cent of the work force did not have a college degree; in 2016, this fraction had reduced to 64 per cent.

The wage of a no-college degree holder in the US has stayed flat at $17.4 for now close to forty years. This is the centrepiece of the evidence around the complaints of Bernie Sanders, Thomas Piketty, Donald Trump, and others—there's been no wage growth, and therefore no income growth, for most of Middle America. But college graduates (BA and above) have increased their wages. Their wage has increased from $26 in 1980 to $32.4 in 2016—an annual growth of 1.1 per cent per annum.

The puzzle is the expanding college wage relative to other wages, especially the near constant high school wage. For those with less than a high school education, there is globalization to blame. These workers are being displaced by workers in the rest of the world. However, there is trouble brewing in college-land—while the US college wage has been increasing, its rate of increase has now slowed considerably post-2000; there's been only a 0.5 per cent annual increase versus double that increase during the previous fifteen years.

This decline in the rate of growth has occurred despite technology expanding at a faster rate. Ordinarily, this should lead to 'excess' demand for a shrinking rate of growth of the 'local' (the US and other AEs) supply of college graduates. But if the world is the market, then local shrinking supply can be replaced by the expanding rest of the world's supply—which is exactly what has been happening. Hence, there is the possibility that college wages may go the way of high school wages, i.e., little or no growth in wages for US college graduates despite significant increases in demand for educated workers. The explanation: the demand for educated workers is increasing, but the supply of educated workers has been expanding significantly faster. But before an empirical explanation, a theoretical (and historical) answer.

Demand and supply: Arthur Lewis meets Gary Becker

One possible explanation for the near constancy of the US college wage is provided by a parallel phenomena in the Rest some sixty years ago. One of the most celebrated articles in the study of developing economies is by Sir Arthur Lewis, titled: 'Economic

Development with Unlimited Supplies of Labour'. This article, published in 1954, outlined the economics behind the observation that the wage of an uneducated worker would stay constant, and close to the minimum wage. The minimum wage was defined as that needed for subsistence. The reason it would not increase was that, at the minimum wage, there would be an unlimited supply of workers willing to work (because of large unemployment or large underemployment). The excess supply prevented the real wage from rising; and subsistence level incomes constrained the wage from going below a minimum subsistence level. This constituted a large part of the developing world circa 1950 and continued till 1980, and indeed, Sir Arthur Lewis was prescient and sharply accurate in his observation.

Now, change the title of Lewis' treatise to 'Development (of the West) with Unlimited Supplies of Skilled Labour' (USSL for brevity) and you will begin to see a pattern.

There are two parallel differences in our Lewis model and Lewis' original model. His model was applicable to the supply of labour within a country, and to unskilled labour. Our model considers the global supply of college-educated labour (the Beckerian spread of education) and the wages of *skilled* labour, particularly labour with a college degree in AEs. In a complete parallel with Lewis, the real wage of a skilled worker in AEs cannot rise too much because an increase in this real wage will be countered by the hiring of the available global supply of skilled workers outside of the AEs (through direct investment abroad).

This direct effect will have an indirect consequence on inflation in AEs since wages are a large fraction of the costs, and hence the price, of a good. But inflation is a monetary phenomenon, so how can a real variable—employment and wages of skilled workers in AEs—affect the price level (inflation) in these economies?

It can. Economists and central bankers have been documenting and analyzing this effect via the Phillips Curve which relates a real variable (unemployment) to inflation. If the velocity of money is low (as it has been for the last decade), then despite monetary expansion, real and nominal wage growth would be approximately equal, i.e., low real wage growth and low inflation will be simultaneously observed.

Testing the USSL model: Can one test the skilled labour version of the Lewis model? Yes. We take the comprehensive tabulation of education data by Barro-Lee as our starting point. Barro-Lee provide two sets of computations about each of the three levels of education—primary, secondary, and tertiary. The two sub-levels are attending and completion. (Tertiary education is the same as college.) Table 7.1 reports the numbers for those who have completed college in the AEs and the Rest.

The excess supply (USSL) is modelled as the percentage difference between the college supply in the West and the Rest, i.e., $(NW_t - NR_t)/NR_t$ where N refers to the number of college graduates in each year t, and W and R refer to the West and Rest, respectively. Now USSL is a variable obtained from education decisions of many individuals around the world and should normally not have a strong effect on US wages.

First, let us look at the world circa 1980—the developed world (West or AEs) had more than one-and-a-half times the magnitude of college workers than the Rest. Between 1980 and 2000, college graduates in the West expanded by 47 million; in the rest of the world the expansion was a larger 104 million. More importantly, during this period (actually in 1992) the absolute number of college graduates in the Rest (81 million) exceeded those in the West (79 million) for the first time. By 2016, the excess supply had

TABLE 7.1: SUPPLY AND WAGES OF COLLEGE-EDUCATED WORKERS, 1960–2016

	1960	1973	1980	1992	2000	2016
Real Wages in the US[1]						
Some College	-	938	880	925	1028	1117
College Graduates	-	1125	1041	1344	1512	1640
Completed College Education *(in millions)*						
US	10.1	19.2	27.4	40.3	45.3	59.9
West	16.5	34.4	50.0	79.1	96.9	124.2
Rest	7.1	19.1	32.5	80.7	136.2	263.1
Gap in Supply of College-Educated Workers[2]						
Ratio (West/Rest)	2.3	1.8	1.5	1.0	0.7	0.5
Percentage difference[3]	132.4	80.1	53.8	-2.0	-28.9	-52.8
Median Inflation in the West (in %)	1.6	8.8	12.3	3.2	2.7	0.4

Source: Barro-Lee (2015); Economic Policy Institute; available at http://www.epi.org/data/#?subject=wage-education

Notes: 1. Wage data sourced from EPI, Bureau of Labor Statistics, in 2016 prices.
2. Aggregate of individuals with completed college degrees (from Barro-Lee Data) is totalled for the West (AEs) and the Rest (all other economies).
3. Percentage difference calculated as 100*(West–Rest)/Rest

reached 139 million; phrased differently, the Rest, today, has more than twice the level of college graduates as the West. Barro-Lee projections for 2030 point to an excess of 280 million college graduates in the Rest—more than three times those in the West. Due to the well known reality of fertility declines, college graduates in the West are not expected to increase by much, just eight million over fourteen years, or simply 570,000 a year.

In contrast, because of the lateness of the demographic transition and the continuing expansion of education, the supply of college graduates in the Rest is projected to increase by 149 million over the next fourteen years, or see an increase of 1.1 million a year. That's half a million versus one million each year for the next fourteen years. In addition, the future will involve some increase in the quality of college education in the Rest, and very little increase in the already existing high quality in the West.

It is this reduction of pressure in the labour market which we believe has been *the* major cause of low growth in US wages. Going forward, and if this linkage holds true, there is very little rise in US college wages in the future.

College graduates in the rest of the world and wages in the US: Empirical evidence

Per capita income in the US has grown at less than 1 per cent per annum for thirty years. For the years 1982–1999, US real wages for college graduates increased at 1.1 per cent per annum; for the next sixteen years (2001–2016), real wage growth was halved for college graduates, to 0.51 per cent per year. GDP growth in the two periods declined from 3.3 per cent to just 1.9 per cent per annum.

Our hypothesis is that the USSL model helps explain most of this decline in the growth of real wages in the US. We haven't yet reached the zero level in growth in real wages (for college graduates), and perhaps never will. But neither was the original Lewis model for unskilled workers about zero growth in real wages; the original insight was, and remains, that when there is excess supply, the real wage gets affected.

Empirical support for the USSL model is presented below in two figures.[35] Figure 7.1 charts the (log) real college wage in the US and excess global supply of college graduates (as defined above). It is not that the US college wage has been constant—it increased at a 1 per cent rate between 1980 and 2000, and has declined to half that rate since. It is not that this rate of growth declined because of the 2008 crisis—real college wages have grown at only 0.52 per cent per annum since 2010. It is the slow, near flat real wage growth for the last twenty-odd years that is of real interest and concern.

FIGURE 7.1: US COLLEGE WAGES EXPLAINED

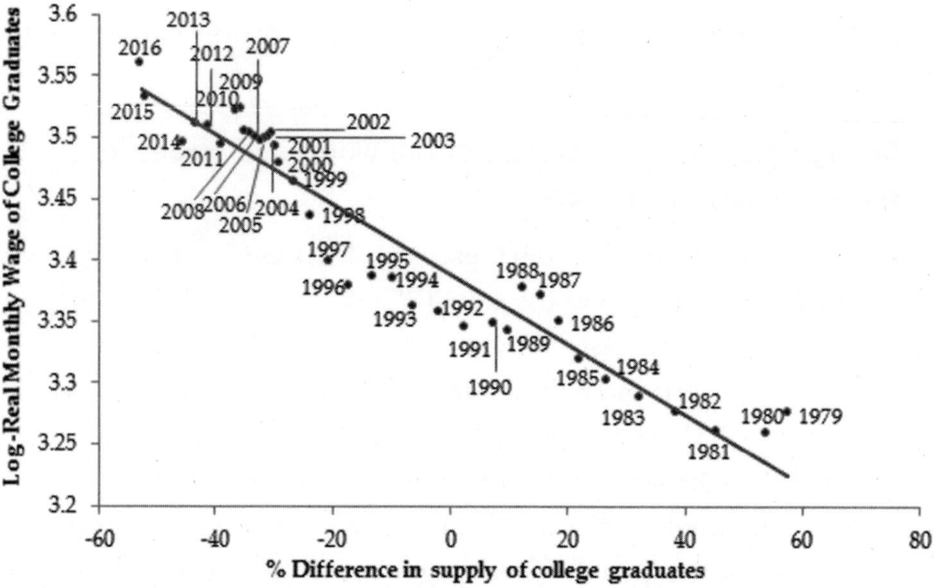

Source: Barro-Lee (2015); Economic Policy Institute, available at http://www.epi.org/data/#?subject=wage-education

What explains the US college wage consistently since 1980 is the increasing supply of college graduates from the Rest. Note that the same model explains the real wage circa 1981, and in 2015; for many years, there is a near perfect prediction. The real US wage is rising, but its rise is tempered by excess supply. The less the relative availability of college graduates in the West, the higher the real wage in the US. This means that college graduates in the West are preferred by employers in the West and the preference is indicated by the higher wage. However, at the margin, it appears that the increase in the US real wage is tempered by the reality of the supply gap.

Flat wages, flat inflation?

That real wage growth is tempered by excess supply is also supported by a direct test of the median inflation in developed economies with respect to various determinants. To reiterate, the linkage is via the impact on wages. Unlike the Phillips Curve formulation, the world is the market, rather than just the local economy. Full employment in the US is not affecting the nominal wage because a non-productivity based increase in the wage will be met by employers either by importing educated labour (the H-1 visa effect) or, failing which, for a little extra cost of production, going overseas and setting up shop—and hiring considerably 'cheaper' labour in comparison.

We have provided above a surprising and logically consistent, explanation for the puzzle of low growth in wages of US college graduates, especially for the period post-1995. The non-college graduate was already receiving a constant wage since the early 1980s; with the wages of skilled workers slowing down markedly, we have the surprising phenomenon of low growth in real wages in the US.

It is likely that the real wage in the rest of the AEs has also been flat for the last twenty-odd years; is USSL an explanation for low inflation in the Western world today? The US Fed Chairperson Janet Yellen recently stated that she (and the Fed) believe that the lack of US inflation is a puzzle, especially when one considers the considerable easing of monetary policy since the financial crisis of 2008.

In addition, the puzzle is exemplified by the fact that the US, is at full and expanding employment (so we should be observing inflation somewhat above 2 per cent than somewhat below)—while the central bank is constantly missing the considerably low target of 2 per cent inflation. But the US monetary authorities were also not able to decipher the underlying cause of low inflation as far back as the mid-1990s.

What happens to the real wage of skilled workers in the rest of the world? If the hiring in the AEs is displaced to the Rest, then does this increased demand lead to a higher real wage? Yes. Is it inflationary? Not in the past decade or so; the gap in median inflation in developing and AEs is close to its lowest level (around 1.6 per cent in 2016 since the 1960s; see Figure 7.2).

The real wages of a skilled worker from the Rest rises because of increased demand, but it is non-inflationary because her real wage is still less than her productivity (measured in PPP terms). And this will continue to happen until her real wage in US dollar is equal to her productivity in PPP $, as is the case with her counterpart in the West. Her wages rise but are below international productivity; the wages of her counterpart in the West do not rise because the wages are already equal to international productivity. This is globalization, but globalization with a difference—this is educated globalization.

After this teaser, we want to take a break. Why flat real wages (a real phenomenon) may lead to low inflation (a monetary phenomenon) is an involved explanation, and one for which it is important to understand the history of inflation, a subject we turn to next.

An all too brief history of the study of inflation

Inflation is one of the most studied topics in the world, and no summary can do the literature justice. Nevertheless, an attempt must be made. One interesting fact is that prior to World War II, the price level, broadly speaking, was a constant, while inflation (change in the price level) was uncertain. An economy experienced price level certainty and inflation uncertainty. Post-1950, the experience has been the opposite—price level uncertainty and inflation certainty.[36] Post-2010, are we going back to the era of price level certainty?

It is this post-WWII Keynesian inflation certainty which has attracted plenty of investigations. Broadly, two explanations have been offered. First is monetarism, which loosely translates to the idea that inflation everywhere and at all times is a monetary phenomenon. Monetary means more money printed—the monetarist expectation was (and is) that excess money printed (excess vis-à-vis the needs of the economy) will go towards increases in the price level, and none will go towards an increase in real output, aka economic growth.

Upsetting the monetarist cart was the reality of the Great Depression and Keynesian economics. Replace money by government, and replace money supply by government deficits, and you have the perfect foil to monetarism—inflation everywhere, and at all times, is a fiscal phenomenon. Of course, real life is a lot more complicated, but you get the drift.

There are zillions of studies on inflation and its determinants. My purpose is to extract from this literature *any implication for the hypothesis that USSL affects inflation in the advanced economies.* And the hypothesis isn't unfounded.

There is inflation caused by food prices rising due to supply shortages, and inflation due to the scarcity of certain commodities at certain times, for e.g., scarcity (or surplus) of oil. Because of the special nature of these goods, central bankers (CBs) and economists like to examine the determinants of core inflation or inflation of goods and services excluding food and fuel. Food and fuel inflation are beyond monetary control, generally determined by the weather and OPEC (Organization of the Petroleum Exporting Countries). Hence, to assess the trend in 'true' inflation, one should only look at core inflation, i.e., inflation in items other than food and fuel.

The biggest determinant of core inflation is wages—if one can explain the trend in wage inflation, one can broadly explain overall inflation. Explanation of wage inflation is what has occupied most minds in the post-war period, and almost all contemporary CBs and their support staff (ordinary economists). If the wage inflation model or explanation involves money variables (e.g., growth in money supply) then one is termed a monetarist; if the explanation is in terms of fiscal deficits, one is classified as a Keynesian.

The most popular offspring of Keynesian economics for inflation is the Phillips Curve, which relates unemployment (a real variable) to inflation (a price variable). The central idea behind the Phillips Curve is that when excess (and symmetrically, deficient) demand is present, it leads to greater (deficient) demand for labour, which leads to lower (higher) unemployment. The increased demand for labour will lead to an increase in wages (because all labour is not available at the same price).

Does the global supply curve slope upward?

The supply curve slopes upward and this causes an increase in wages, and if this increase in wages is not matched by an increase in productivity, then there is wage inflation, which leads to an increase in core inflation, and which, therefore, leads to an increase in headline inflation.

An upward-sloping supply curve is not an easily understood concept. And I can tell this from experience. My undergraduate degree was in electrical engineering, and before transiting to economics via a degree in public and international affairs, I worked as a computer-aided design engineer in Silicon Valley (yes, literally, when that baby was being born in the late 1960s). As an engineer, I believed that everything was replicable; hence, the supply curve was *not* upward-sloping, it was flat. If one plant had 100 workers, an increase in demand would lead to the building of another plant, also employing 100 workers. All materials and labour would cost the same. I was just replicating, so what was the problem in this? My fellow student and colleague at the Woodrow Wilson School, Princeton University (and since then a close friend), Suman Bery, enlightened me about the joys of economics and tactfully explained that the supply curve was indeed upward-sloping, and that I should go read Joan Robinson on the subject. (Apart from being very smart, Suman was also an Oxford graduate.)

I did read Robinson, and her essay on the supply curve was brilliant and sublime. And the upward-sloping supply curve has remained unchanged in my opinion—until now. Recall that Sir Arthur Lewis postulated that the supply curve was flat for unskilled labour, and here I am, almost fifty years later, suggesting, and trying to prove, that the supply curve for skilled labour, too, has *today* become relatively flat, and hence real wages are relatively flat, leading (indirectly) to the result of inflation being at a low level (and flat).

Getting back to the Phillips Curve, we are nearing the end of this detour. Part of the increase in demand leads to an increase in wages and prices, and part to an increase in employment. If an economy is at full employment, all increased demand would lead to wage inflation. Correspondingly, if there is excess unemployment (as during the Great Depression), none of the increase in demand would lead to inflation; rather, all excess demand would lead to increased employment, and increased output, and zero wage inflation (since a lot of excess workers are waiting to be employed and will be willing to work at the existing wage).

Note how the various esoteric economic terms all refer to the same simple description of the relationship between a real variable and inflation, for e.g., output gap, potential versus actual output, excess demand, non-linearity in the relationship between unemployment and inflation, etc. The higher the gap between actual and potential output, the less any expansionary policy would lead to inflation. This theory, or belief, or reality has guided CBs for the better part of the last fifty years. Strict monetarism, or the belief that the knowledge of money supply matters for inflation, was tossed out of the window the same day in 1984 that the US Fed stopped announcing the latest weekly money supply figures, at 4.15 pm, on Thursday afternoons.

The great inflation decline (GID)

Today, we are back to the low inflation era of the 1950s and 1960s. For the seventeen years following 1951, Consumer Price Index (CPI) inflation in the US averaged 1.7 per cent, and the medium inflation in the AEs averaged 2.8 per cent. For the years 2000–2016, US inflation was 2.1 per cent, and in AEs, 1.9 per cent. In Figure 7.2, the two lines represent the median rate of inflation in AEs and in emerging markets.

Inflation jumped in the world in 1972 due to a wheat shortage, and the Yom Kippur war of October 1973 induced double-digit world inflation—the first time in world history, and very likely the last time. Oil prices quadrupled in 1973 and the world experienced

**FIGURE 7.2: LOW INFLATION IS MORE THAN TWENTY YEARS OLD—
MEDIAN INFLATION (1960-2016)**

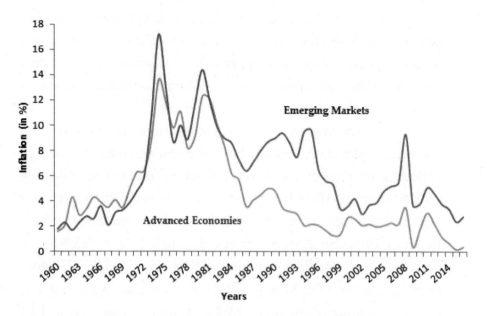

Source: World Economic Outlook, IMF (2017); author computations.

a phenomenon which came to be known as 'stagflation'—a word invented to describe low output growth and high inflation, something neither the monetarists nor the Keynesians thought possible.

Then came Paul Volcker who fought inflation, and won. Volcker was brought in by President Carter to head the US Fed in 1979, with the near explicit mandate to fight double-digit inflation. This, he did. In fact, he was so successful and popular that Republican President Reagan reappointed him in 1983. Volcker's second term came to an end in August 1987. No necessary causation here, but less than two months after his leaving, the US stock market crashed by 25 per cent in one day.

By 1984, OPEC inflation had run its course. From double-digit inflation for most of the period from 1973 to 1983, median inflation in the AEs was reduced to 6.2 per cent in 1984 and 5.7 per cent in 1985. From the early 1990s, median inflation has stayed well below 4 per cent and close to 2 per cent. This is what can be termed the 'great inflation decline' (GID), and it's a phenomenon crying out for an explanation.

Economists have tried various explanations for the GID. My favourite explanation is also a favourite among many economists, including officials of the Reserve Bank of India. The reasoning centres around a three-letter word—oil—as it did forty-five years ago. But has oil mattered for inflation since the early 1980s? Between 1998 and 2007, oil prices quintupled (from US $14.4 a West Texas intermediate barrel in 1998 to US $72 in 2007, before peaking at around US $160 in 2008), and inflation in the AEs and in a large number of emerging market economies was *lower* by half a percentage point.

Today, the US economy is as close to full employment as it has ever been, and yet there is no sign of inflation. The GID has caused the central banks in the world to fight a different and unprecedented battle—how to increase the inflation rate. Over the last few years, central banks (the Fed, ECB, and the Bank of Japan) are fighting, clamouring, plotting, and begging to get the inflation rate *up* to 2 per cent, and 'obviously' not succeeding. What could be the reason?

The reason is that the world has changed, and the old models do not fit the facts of the new world. And the world changed more than twenty years ago. Misinterpreting this change or not acknowledging it has led central bankers to make big policy mistakes. One such prominent central banker was Alan Greenspan.

How one central banker misinterpreted the great inflation decline

In February 1995, barely two months after the large Mexican currency devaluation of December 1994, Fed Chairman Alan Greenspan raised interest rates in the US by a half percentage point to 6 per cent. For the uninitiated, half a per cent (50 basis points) is a very large move by the US Fed and not that usual with inflation hovering around 3 per cent.

Greenspan was wrong on at least two counts. First, he could not conceive that a large Mexican devaluation of December 1994, affecting at least all of Latin America and most of the East, would or should have an impact on US inflation, and consequently on the US monetary policy and its fight to keep inflation low. Traditional monetary policy was fast declining as an instrument for attacking inflation even then.

The second error of the redoubtable Greenspan was in thinking that inflation in the US was a problem. In 1994, consumer prices had increased by 2.6 per cent, having increased by a seemingly large 3 per cent the year before. What Greenspan was apparently attempting to attack was not inflation, but future impending inflation to be brought upon by the higher than inflation-neutral GDP growth in the future. That is a mouthful (my apologies) but it gets to the heart of the puzzle, and how the central bankers have adamantly refused to see the Lewis-Mach II writing on the wall (explained below). In 1994 GDP growth in the US was a high 4 per cent and Greenspan (wrongly) inferred that this high growth would induce higher inflation.

It is instructive to see how un-right or un-prescient the leading central banker in the world was about future US events. In 1995, the year of the great strike against impending inflation, US GDP growth recorded 2.7 per cent, and would not record lower GDP growth until the 9–11 year. For the next five years (1996–2000), US GDP growth averaged 4.3 per cent per annum; US CPI inflation averaged 2.5 per cent per annum. During the previous decade US GDP growth averaged 3.1 per cent, and US inflation 3.6 per cent. This was the first warning sign that ignoring higher education (skilled labour) in the developing world would lead to domestic policy mistakes.

Explaining the great inflation decline: The usual suspects fail

As Figure 7.2 showed, low inflation has been a phenomenon for the last twenty years. That is what we have to seek an explanation for. Topping the list of claimants seeking credit for low inflation, you guessed it, are central banks. These central banks are now more independent of government restraints (and constraints) than ever before, and *surely* this institutional change has helped decrease inflation. The number of inflation-targeting countries has also increased, and these born-again inflation hawks fight even non-existent inflation with the tenacity of a raging bull. Hence, inflation is low because of sensible central bank policies.

Are there other princes vying for the throne? Not many; the fiscal deficits theory of inflation is not taken seriously any more, nor is the money supply variant. The rejection is on the same grounds—the theory does not fit the facts. High and low fiscal deficits (look at Greece and India, both with high fiscal deficits and low inflation) are irrelevant for predicting inflation; the Phillips Curve also does not work any longer, and neither does the newest inflation kid on the block—the Taylor rule—which advocates and explains the setting of policy interest rates on the basis of inflation gaps and output gaps. As Monty Python's John Cleese's dead parrot might say, Keynesians and monetarists are no more; they have ceased to predict inflation, they are discredited, tired, and retired; theirs are ex-models of inflation, they have gone to their keeper (history books).

Low inflation: Demography to the rescue

A more convincing explanation is offered by those who argue that the changing demographics of the world are responsible for low inflation. Demographic change is commonly measured as the percentage change in the population aged between fifteen and sixty-four—this is the group that supports the dependents aged less than fifteen or more than sixty-four years of age. If the size of this group declines, there are fewer workers in the economy, and hence less income and less demand, *ceteris paribus* again. Less demand means lower inflation. Put differently, fertility is down and population growth has slowed; there are fewer mouths to feed, fewer people to demand goods and services, and hence lower inflation. On the other side, an ageing population in AEs can add to inflation pressures because now this section of the population is richer, and can afford more ageing services.

Many such demographic models have been estimated and a fair summary is that the decline in the dependency ratio (the percentage of population between the ages of fifteen and sixty-four) has had a persistent (and statistically significant) effect on Western inflation. Ageing, however, has not turned up, as a consistent, significant explanation for the puzzle of low inflation as yet.

Low inflation: A horse race among competing models

That low inflation in the AEs is well explained by the 'excess' supply of college graduates is supported by a horse race among competing models (regression analysis involving 'competing' horses for the prize of explaining low inflation). What one is attempting to explain is the median inflation rate in AEs post the 1970s. The competing explainers include the median fiscal deficit in AEs, and two demographic variables for the AEs: growth in the population aged between fifteen and sixty-four years, and growth in population aged above sixty-four years.

FIGURE 7.3: ACTUAL AND USSL PREDICTED INFLATION IN AEs

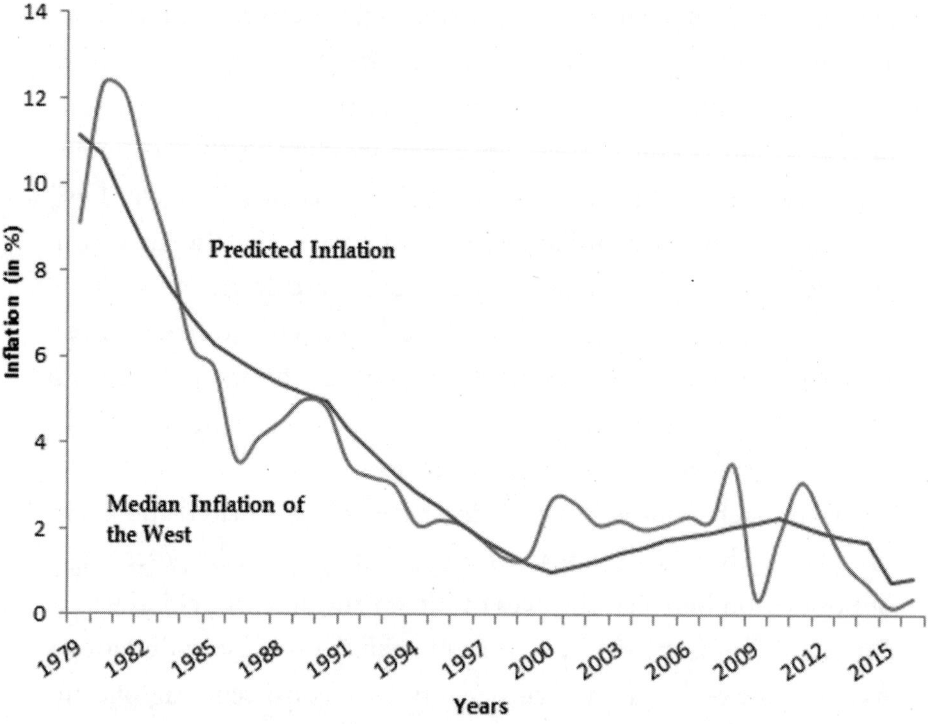

Source: World Economic Outlook, IMF (2017); Barro-Lee (2015); author computations.

The results: the explainer with the lowest statistical significance (actually none at all) is fiscal deficits—this much-touted Keynesian variable, and the subject of hundreds of learned articles, explains precious little about the great inflation decline.

The demographic variables are significant, especially the dependency ratio. By itself, this explains about 36 per cent of the median inflation between 1984 and 2016. By itself, the elderly variable is also statistically significant, but can explain only 17 per cent of the variation. The less said about the presumed association between median fiscal deficits and median CPI inflation in the AEs, the better. There's no explanation whatsoever in a stand-alone model. The USSL supply gap is very significant, and it alone explains 74 per cent of the variation. All the variables added up explain an additional 6 per cent to 80 per cent—that is the amount of extra information which we can learn from demography.

Figure 7.3 plots the model predicted median inflation in developed economies on the basis of the college supply gap and a time trend. Note the closeness of the relationship between the two, and note how exogenous (another favourite word of economists loosely meaning 'out of the system') the USSL measure is. Monetarism, Keynesianism, inflation targeting, fiscal deficits—none of the traditional arguments work.

The uncertain future

As of today, what we do know is that labour earnings in the West have been relatively flat over the last twenty years. What about the next twenty? This is where forecasts become tricky, especially given the uncertain future. More seriously, because of education and technological advances, and the strong interdependence between the two, extrapolating from the past may not be as accurate. Artificial intelligence, robots, 3D printing—name it what you will, that will be an important part of society and bring about non-linear changes.

Barro-Lee provide estimates of college graduates for 2030, but these may not turn out to be accurate. Even the limited expansion of college graduates in the AEs may not take place. There is a double whammy here for the West (and likely for the East as well)—costs of college education have increased, and are increasing, at a faster pace than inflation. At the same time, the returns, in the form of income growth, are declining. Add a third facet—jobs will become scarcer. This mix suggests a 'correction' in the college market— less students, less expansion, and the net result might be both an increase in earnings for those with jobs, and a decline in overall employment of college graduates in the world.

It is likely, therefore, that societies will have to revisit the basic income concept, for e.g., a guaranteed minimum income for all, a subject we take up in some detail in Chapter 10.

8

The Future is Women: Women and Transformation

These boots are made for walkin'
And that's just what they'll do
One of these days these boots are gonna walk all over you
Are you ready boots?
Start walkin'!

—These Boots Are Made for Walkin' *by* Nancy Sinatra
(*lyrics by* Lee Hazelwood, Boots, 1966)

No matter what the definition of equality between men and women, it surely is the case that women are more equal than men today than at any time in human history. Notice that I said 'more equal', not 'equal'. It is also the case that the fight for justice for women is more vocal today than at any time in human history. Is there a contradiction there? Not really, but it does suggest that the subject deserves a closer examination.

Going back a few centuries or even just a few decades, what is observed is that men are considered physically stronger, and are in a significant majority, and control most, if not all, positions of power and influence. Perhaps coincidentally, it is observed that women, on average, have less education than men.

Consider the data on college completion in the Western[37] world—the region that has been the most advanced in providing education to women. In 1870, the earliest year for which Barro-Lee provides the data, less than five women had *completed* college relative to 100 men that had done so. By 1913, this ratio had increased to 53 per cent.

Again, to put numbers in perspective, a century ago (in 1913), the West was inhabited by 680 million individuals, and only six million had *attended* college, out of which four million were men and 1.9 million women, yielding the result that for every 100 men attending college, there were only forty-eight women who did so. Traversing through history, this ratio had more than doubled by

2010, such that in that last year of Barro-Lee data, college women outnumbered men by 11 per cent, i.e., for every 100 men attending college, there were 111 women doing so. No doubt when this number is updated (2017), this fraction will be higher and the future course of Western history will likely be of men catching up with women—and that will be for the first time since Eve.

Of course, higher education is not the only determinant of success in the marketplace or in politics. But what else is there, and I ask that only half-facetiously. You will rightly counter that merit is important, as is age and experience. That, of course, cannot be disagreed. But economists have learnt to adjust for easily measurable factors like age (and experience) in their models. So what they rightly compare is the 'adjusted' or 'equivalent' wage profiles for men and women with similar profiles of education and experience. In addition, there is no reason to think that men and women have different *average* abilities for the same education level.

So where does that leave us? With the great education transformation, it is women in the driver's seat. But will they be *allowed* that 'privilege'? Likely not without a fight, but Mother Nature will prevail, as she always does.[38]

The great fertility decline

Woman does not live by bread alone, though progress can be measured by how much less the woman is baking today. The great fertility decline happened in the Western world in the 19th century (see Clarke, 2005). Between 1800 and 1913, the total fertility rate in France dropped from 4.4 to 2.5; for the UK, the decline was from 5 to 2.9; and for Germany, the drop was from 5.4 to 3.5. Economists only discovered the value of education post-Becker, though like gold, the value of a good or service does not depend on its discovery by economists.

While women lagged considerably behind men in terms of higher (college or tertiary) education, there was less inequality in overall achievement in schooling. In 1870, women in the West had an average of 1.2 years of schooling compared to 1.6 years for the men. In contrast, in 1870, average educational attainment for women in the non-Western world was zero years, compared to 0.01 years for men. And this goes a long distance towards explaining why the demographic transition (fewer kids and lower population growth) took a lot longer to arrive in the developing world.

It is believed that history would have been kinder if somehow the poor countries had been able to control their population growth. A centuries old phenomenon, associated with all countries, is that with development, fertility rates (number of children ever born per woman) declines, and labour force participation of women increases, and both fuel each other. This is indeed what has happened in China, India, and most developing countries. The fertility rate in India in 2000 was three births per woman; in Bangladesh, about the same; and in China and Iran, less than two births per woman. The fertility rate in India, circa 2016, is as follows—the replacement rate is 2.1 children per woman, and this is heading south. Population growth rate in India today is close to 1.1 per cent per annum, whereas in China, primarily because of a forced one-child policy, it is only 0.4 per cent per annum. The new story in the world today is not population growth, but the great fertility decline. If it hasn't yet arrived in your favourite poor country, it is arriving soon.

Note the virtuous cycle—more education for women means a lower demand for the number of children, and a higher demand for the quality (of life offered). A higher quality of life means the sons and daughters will have more education than otherwise; they, in turn, will demand fewer children. The demand for children is unlikely to be zero, but likely to converge between 1 and 2, which is where the Western world is today.

Women and discrimination

There is more than a lively debate about equal wages for equal work and equal ability. And if the wages are not equal, then we have a convincing display of the muscle power of irrational men. Note what happens when there is discrimination in the marketplace. The owner, in this case the male, will be losing *profits* if he decides to discriminate (whether the discrimination is on the basis of sex, or race, or nationality is irrelevant).

There are two examples of how discrimination[39] takes place, and it is important to distinguish between the two. One example of discrimination in the marketplace is that I decide not to hire a woman at all, and instead, that job is occupied by a male, at presumably a higher wage than the female. This is an irrational and costly decision by all means.

Now let us consider the alternative. I am super-rational, and I hire a woman who is just as productive as a man, but I pay her lower wages. In this instance, I end up making extra profits, and the woman gets paid less than is her due. This is the reason behind many arguing for equal pay for equal work.

But can the latter instance happen for a large number of women, and on a sustainable basis? If all employers only hire women at a lower wage, then they have to be explicitly, or implicitly, colluding. Is that happening? This seems unlikely, but one should look at the evidence. What one finds, in the case of the US, is that the average wages of women are only three-fourths the average wages of men. That is the situation at present; in 1980, however, that ratio was less than 60 per cent.

Considerable evidence exists that women today have an edge over men in terms of educational attainment. Obtaining only 75 per cent for similar, or higher, educational levels is a definite sign of discrimination. This 'fact' also shows that the most capitalist of economies, the US, is composed of very rational employers who are clearly colluding to make profits off the backs of women.

Fortunately, this 'fact' is plain fiction. Several scholars (and a large number of female economists) have documented that discrimination against women is not an empirical reality in the US, circa 2000. Writing in the economics journal *American Economic Review* in May 2003, June O'Neill concludes that a substantial portion of the wage gap of 25 percentage points (the difference between the $100 the average male employee gets and the $75 the average female employee is able to garner) is due to work experience and occupational choice. She also argues that women have less work experience because they withdraw from the labour force to bear and look after children; and they are dominantly in occupations where the wage is lower, for both men and women. When O'Neill factors in these differences, the wage gap is reduced to only 10 per cent. The author also notes that wage differences vary by the level of education; and that the wage gap falls considerably (to near zero) when the examination is restricted to only high school graduates.

The major conclusion from several such studies is the same: there is precious little discrimination in the marketplace. The discrimination that exists, and it does, is outside of the market and inside the home.

As a young undergraduate at Purdue in the mid-1960s, 'fresh off the boat' from India, I noticed what appeared to me to be very strange—there were very few professional women in America. Even in India, a poor developing economy with a lot of discrimination against women, female doctors, and lawyers, and teachers were not uncommon and secretarial jobs were occupied mostly by men.

In many ways, that casual inference was not incorrect; what research has demonstrated is that occupational choice accounts for a large portion of the wage gap between men and women, and many women were in low-paying occupations in the mid-1960s. Today, increasingly, women are more broadly represented.

Indeed, times are changing, perhaps because women are ascending. Governments are changing their policies on leave when children are born; some Scandinavian countries (and others will follow) require parental leave to be shared between both mother and father. This will have the strong implication that differences in job experience will no longer be an important factor in explaining the female–male wage gap.

While on wage gap, and since I'm an avid sports fan, the question of equal pay for female and male cricketers, basketball players, golfers, etc. keeps coming up. Wives, sisters, and daughters are particularly vocal on this score. In one such heated discussion, my daughter herself came up with the following observation: should a male model be paid the same as Gisele Bundchen? She couldn't quite bring herself to say yes—and neither could I.

Far removed from the developed world of the US is the developing economy of India. In 1983, in urban India, for the ages between fifteen and twenty-four, it was observed that young women had two-thirds of the earnings of young men. Many in India, especially women scholars and economists who lean left, attributed this to a discriminating marketplace. On deeper examination, it was observed that the education levels of young women were two-thirds of young men. Once again, the lower female wage had more to do with discrimination at home than with discrimination in the marketplace. In a society such as India, which has historically favoured sons over daughters, parents preferred to send their sons to school; family income was overspent on the young men, possibly to attract higher future income in the form of a dowry.

But even India is changing, and changing fast. A parallel 2011 household survey found that young women and young men in urban India had the same levels of education; and female wages were 3 per cent higher. The 'market' stayed the same—what changed was the discriminatory behaviour at home.

Discrimination at home: Sex ratio at birth

Yet another example of societal preferences being skewed in favour of males is provided by the data on the low sex ratio at birth in several developing economies, and especially in India and China.

One of the most important stylized facts is the near constancy of the sex ratio at birth—for a 'social' variable, its near constancy across space and time is comparable to scientific constants like the acceleration of gravity. This unusual 'factoid' is extensively documented by Brian and Jaisson (2007). The authors' exhaustive review of historical studies documents that estimates of the sex ratio at birth have captivated some of the greatest statistical and mathematical minds over the last three hundred years. Whether it is Laplace, Poisson, Bernoulli, Darwin or Gini, all have at one time or another engaged in documenting and verifying the stylized fact of the sex ratio at birth. What each study found, and re-established, was that the probability of a child being a boy was close to 51.3 per cent—yes, more boys are born than girls. A probability of male birth of 51.3 per cent translates into a sex ratio at birth of 105.3.[40] This simply meant that 105 boys are born for every 100 girls, across time, space, and continents. (Among blacks, the constant is close to 104.)

Over time, this constant gravitates towards 100—equal number of boys and girls. This happens because boys have a higher infant and child mortality rate than girls. Men *are* the weaker sex.

In boy-preferring societies like India and China, technology has allowed the sex ratio at birth to be much higher than 105. Parents abort the girl foetus, and thus, defy Mother Nature. However, in another example where Mother Nature always wins, both India and China are reverting to the biological sex ratio at birth, India faster than China. In ten years, India is expected, by some,[41] to achieve the natural parity at birth, i.e., parents are expected to not abort the girl child, because the perceived worth of a girl child is increasing.

Discrimination against girls is a major social issue even today, and comes to the fore through everyday examples. For instance, recall the TV appeal of Harmanpreet Kaur's mother to parents asking them not to abort the girl child. This happened when Ms Kaur scored a blistering 171 to help seal India's entry into the final of the Women's Cricket World Cup, 2017.

There are two other examples suggesting that the transfer of power to women is more reality than hype. These are two very disparate examples, and at opposite ends of the spectrum. The first example is that of corporate boards; the second example has to do with the improving scores of women in SAT exams, and the constancy of male scores. This is another good omen surrounding the ascent of women.

Board seats for women

One of the most cited statistics on discrimination against women (and by implication, that progress for them seems muted) is their lack of representation in corporate boardrooms. Since 2011, this comprehensive list is being published by Deloitte. For 2016, the most recent data reports on boardroom fractions (i.e., the percentage of women who are on the board of directors of corporations) for forty-four countries, equally divided between the West and the Rest.

Let us first examine some quick information revealed by the data. On an average, only 16 per cent of board seats are held by women overall, and a slightly higher percentage—21 per cent—by women in the West. For the US, the percentage is a low 14.2 per cent, very close to the median of 15 per cent. The raw percentages suggest that in the boardrooms of the world there is active discrimination.

However, the fraction of board seats, while useful, is not that good a metric of discrimination in the market. Assume for a moment (an assumption that seems eminently reasonable) that a college degree is a necessary condition for being on a board. In addition, you need to have worked in the market (rather than have been a house-wife or a house-husband) to satisfy the 'minimum' requirements for appointment. Hence, the metric one really wants is the percentage of women on boards *after adjusting for higher education and labour force participation*.

Women have equal if not more education than men, and their labour force participation rates in Western economies are very high—on equal merit basis, women should comprise close to 40 per cent of board membership. Only 15 per cent is akin to highway (male) robbery.

The results of this exercise are reported in Table 8.1, and ranked from the most women-friendly (and in the current context, the fairest country) to the most misogynistic.

TABLE 8.1: CORPORATE BOARDROOMS—DO THEY SEX-DISCRIMINATE?

		Proportion of Women on Boards (%)		Difference (%)
Rank	Country	Actual	Potential	(Potential–Actual)
1	India	12.4	11	10
2	France	40.0	39	3
3	South Africa	19.5	24	-19
4	Norway	42.0	53	-20
7	Turkey	11.5	17	-34
8	Sweden	31.7	53	-40
11	Germany	19.5	35	-45
13	United Kingdom	20.3	42	-51
15	Malaysia	13.7	29	-52
16	Australia	20.4	45	-54
24	Canada	17.7	46	-62
27	United States	14.2	43	-67
28	China	10.7	37	-71
30	Indonesia	7.9	30	-74
33	Mexico	6.0	28	-79
35	Chile	6.5	34	-81
36	Brazil	7.7	45	-83
37	Russia	5.8	39	-85
38	Japan	4.1	35	-88
39	South Korea	2.5	32	-92

Source: Deloitte: Women in Boardrooms; World Development Indicators, World Bank; Barro-Lee (2015); author's calculations.

Note: Potential is estimated on the basis of the relative number of working female college graduates to the corresponding number for men. For e.g., in the US, while only 14.2 per cent of the boards have women, 43 per cent are eligible to be on the board.

The country with the least discrimination against women is India; France is the only other country which discriminates 'positively', if there's such a thing. Despite that, only 12 per cent of the board seats in India are occupied by women.

Is this result plausible? India is widely believed to be a misogynistic country, and one deserving that description based on its sex ratio at birth. However, as Joan Robinson famously said, whatever be the conclusion on India, the opposite is also true. India is also a classic case of discrimination at home, but not so much in the marketplace. The unadjusted data shows India as having only 12.4 per cent board seats occupied by women; but India has traditionally had discrimination in schools, and the number of women participating in the workforce is much less than it should be—only 26 per cent compared to the 50–60 per cent participation rate in most countries. In 2010, only a third of college graduates in India were women, though the situation is fast-changing for the younger cohorts, where the numbers of college graduates are near equal.

The real surprise (in addition to India) is the US—on an untouched by human hands (UBHH) basis, only 14 per cent of board seats were occupied by women; potentially, women should have occupied 43 per cent of the seats. In the list of forty-four countries, the US ranks a low twenty-seventh—well behind the UK which holds the thirteenth place.

The point of this exercise is both to illustrate that all is not necessarily well with the world, and to suggest that change for the better is rapidly taking place. Between 2011 and 2016, on a population-weighted basis, the gender gap in boardrooms improved from 27 per cent to 34 per cent. Now for the next ten years . . .

SAT scores: Women improving

In addition to near equal salary levels, there is another very hopeful sign for the relative advancement of women. Whether it is Spelling Bee contests in the US or competitive exams for admission to government jobs, trends are showing that the new and now toppers are women; at a minimum, there is an increasing *frequency* of women toppers. And data on SAT scores in the US can substantiate this trend. Given the increasing attraction of American universities over the last decade or so, and attraction for the best and brightest students, the SAT data can shed light on how much women are doing better than men (or vice versa).

The trend is clear. In the top group (scores in the 700–800 range) women have equal representation with men for verbal aptitude; particularly in Math, there is a significant improvement since 1996.

TABLE 8.2: WOMEN SHARING SPACE AT THE TOP

	Percentage in the 700–800 Range			
Year	**Reading**		**Maths**	
	Male	*Female*	*Male*	*Female*
1996	50.5	49.5	67.4	32.6
2000	49.1	50.9	65.8	34.3
2005	51.0	49.0	64.2	35.9
2010	46.2	53.8	62.9	37.1
2016	47.8	52.3	61.5	38.5

Source: College Board, SAT Data Tables.

Note: Ratios calculated as a proportion of the total who scored in the 700–800 range.

The top bracket contained 32.6 per cent women in 1996; in 2016, this percentage was 6 percentage points higher, a sharp increase for this very slow moving ratio. The only conclusion which can be drawn is this—the future is women.

The great education catch-up

If there is one chart that captures the rapid strides that women have made (and are making), it is Figure 8.1. This figure documents the female/male ratio in the three stages of education, as well as in aggregate years of education. The primary school education story was over by the mid-1980s, i.e., in the aggregate, girls were equal to boys (and exceeding them), going by the numbers pursuing primary education. The number is above 100 because of the backlog in some countries like India where 'overaged' girls were going to primary school, when they should have been in secondary school.

The sharpest increase in the participation of women has happened in the all-important tertiary sector. In the mid-1970s, for every ten men who attended college, seven women did the same. In 2014, this number was above a 100 for the world. To repeat: at the world level, more women were attending college than men in 2014. More of these women will work in the future than the present (primarily because fertility rates decline with educational achievement) and women with college degrees participate in workspaces at a higher rate than those with a secondary education. This will mean that women will be equal, if not the major breadwinners, in highly educated households. If that isn't a sign of an impending social revolution, then what is?

**FIGURE 8.1: THE GREATEST OF ALL CATCH-UPS—FEMALE TO MALE
RATIO IN TERMS OF EDUCATION**

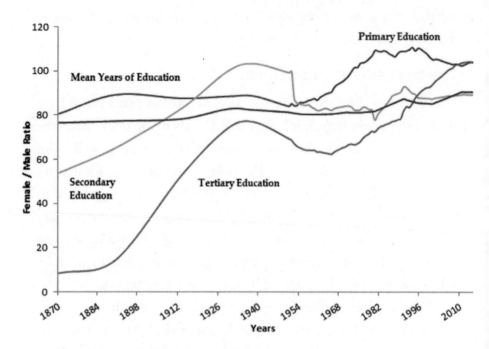

Source: Barro-Lee (2015); author computations.

Note: For each category (e.g., mean years of education, educational attainment at different levels), the graph represents the ratio of female attainment to that of the male.

9

Education Makes the World Equal

A star lit up like a cigar
Strung out like a guitar
Maybe you can educate my mind
Explain all these controls
Can't sing but I've got soul
The goal is elevation

—Elevation *by* U2
(*lyrics by* Bono, All That You Can't Leave Behind, 2000)

Some call it the economics of envy, while others term it the root of all evil. Either way, for the last nearly 200 years, discussions about inequality have played an important part in policy formulation. In Marxian England of the 1850s, a very large fraction of the population was illiterate (upwards of 80 per cent); the Gini index of income inequality was in the mid-50s, and a third of the population was living below a dollar a day. Inequality and poverty were the *same*. But that was then.

The world has just witnessed one of the biggest declines in world inequality. The world Gini was at a level of 62.5 in 2016, just within kissing distance of the level observed nearly 150 years ago in 1870—61.9. Yet, I would wager any money that all the articles you read are about how world inequality has increased beyond most people's imagination, and why these are the days of the Armageddon for the bottom 99 per cent of the world.

There is a basis for this inflamed and incorrect view of what is happening. It is that inequality in the most advanced (and most media influential) economy in the world, the US, is at its highest level ever, at least since 1820, which is as far back as data goes. This largest Gini, at 57.9, is higher than the 1870 level of 54.1, and also higher than the 1980 level of 44.1.[42] Inequality in the other world media economy, the UK, peaked in 2008 at 49.3, and has come down sharply post the great financial crisis to 44.4—the same level where it was in 1993. The UK Gini today is also near identical to the 43.2 level observed in 1820.

There is no doubt that inequality in the US is at a disturbingly high level. However, income concentration in the US (or the UK, or even China) may tell us precious little, and may indeed misinform us, about trends in world inequality. Going back to the Rawlsian theme introduced in Chapter 2, the question that arises is—whose inequality? Should we focus on the inequality in a rich US, or even the former colonial power UK, together accounting for 200 million (or less than 3 per cent) of the world's population, or should we celebrate the declining inequality amongst the other seven billion individuals? The answer depends largely on your perspective and/ or ideology.

The changes in world inequality can be explained by that old MIT/Harvard joke: When an economist leaves the MIT department to get a job at Harvard, he raises the average IQ in both places. Analogously, if the average income of an American increases by 1 per cent, and that of the average non-American by 4 per cent (warning: this is not a joke), then world inequality lowers.

This can be explained using simple incontrovertible facts— no PPP dollars, just plain greenbacks. In 1980, China and India together had 45 per cent of the world's population, where the world consists of the 137 countries for which the IMF provides data for US dollar exchange rates. The combined share of the two countries in global dollar income was 4.5 per cent, close to an all-time low (see Chapter 4). Per capita income for the populations in these two very poor economies, containing over 80 per cent of the world's absolute poor was US $286 a year or 78 cents a day. Per capita income in the rest of the world was US $4990 a year or US $13.7 a day, in other words eighteen times the income of the very poor Chinese/Indian (hereafter CI).

Fast forward to 2016, the poor CI has an annual income of

US $4980, registering a compound annual growth of 7.9 per cent, in US dollars, for thirty-six years. Per capita income in the other 135 countries is now US $16000 a year, with a compound annual growth of 3.2 per cent a year. The growth in income of an average individual in the advanced and rich economies was 4 per cent a year between 1950 and 1980. The population of these advanced and rich economies in 1980 was 760 million. The number of very poor in China and India in 1980, on the other hand, stood at a staggering 1.7 billion.

No matter how you slice the data—PPP terms, US dollar terms, or local currency terms, or in terms of food, or refrigerators, or cars, or electricity consumption, or life expectancy, or education, or any variant thereof—you cannot change the simple result that inequality *in the world* is down, really down. So it remains a mystery why the outpourings of concern for world inequality, among the intelligentsia (including redoubtable institutions like the World Bank and the IMF) and/or the purveyors of envy, are at their highest levels, even more than in Marx's England of 1850.

Both China and India should be prominent in this discussion, especially China. Given the relative size of the two economies, much of what happens in these two countries affects wages, profits, growth, and inequality everywhere else. It is likely that with each Gini point of inequality *increase* within China, world inequality probably *decreased* by a proportional amount. It is crucial to recognize and emphasize this fact. *As the poor gain income in India and China, and as the middle classes and rich in these countries grow at a faster pace than their rich country counterparts, world inequality declines.*

Let me recount the theory behind the expectation that inequality has to worsen in the large developing world first, before improving once these countries become developed or rich.

The search for the meaning of inequality:
Kuznets Curve and beyond

In 1955, just a few years before Becker revolutionized thinking about the determination of income, Nobel laureate Simon Kuznets, in a paper titled 'Economic Growth and Income Inequality' postulated that as part of the development process, the income distribution in a country would first worsen, and then improve, i.e., the relationship between inequality (y-axis) and per capita income (x-axis) could be represented by an inverted-U. The economic reason for this expected move was broadly the following: the development process is synonymous with the decline of traditional agriculture and the consequent rise of industry. Traditional agriculture is rural, and has mostly unskilled workers, whereas the industrial worker is urban, has slightly more skill, and works with a greater amount of capital than his rural counterpart. Hence, understandably, his income is more than that of the agricultural worker. The share of agriculture declines over time. This is one of the very true stylized facts of development. Both India and China have less than a 17 per cent share of agriculture in GDP today, while both had this share upwards of 40 to 60 per cent circa 1950 or even 1980.

Hence, Kuznets reasoned that as labour migrated to industry, it would receive higher wages because of higher productivity; a small fraction of the population growing at a faster than average rate meant that inequality would worsen. Over time, and as the share of agriculture moved close to an irreducible minimum, the system would be in reverse, and hence inequality would improve.

This hypothesis set off a flurry of research and we are now past the 60th anniversary, and counting. There has been significant research and insignificant findings[43]—on the existence of the

Kuznets Curve, that is. Several tests of the Kuznets Curve have confirmed its validity; several others have rejected it.[44]

However, the very sensible future forecast by Kuznets (and almost every other prominent economist) did not happen. World inequality has now been declining for close to fifty years (since 1972) and is today at a level last seen in 1870. A legitimate question which arises here is: why did the whole class fail? In one word, and being unavoidably repetitious, what happened was 'education'.

As we have repeatedly pointed out, education is a great equalizing force, possibly the greatest such force. Equalization of education, or near equalization if you prefer, has been the countervailing force that has proven Kuznets (and others) wrong. In 1950, the world Gini for education years[45] was above 66 (almost equal to income inequality Gini); in 2016, it had more than halved to 33; by 2030, the Gini for education is expected to decline by another 12 per cent. Can declining income inequality be far behind?

The analysis presented above would also seem to reject the Kuznets Curve, but its hold is quite pervasive. As Peter Lindert observed, 'The Kuznets Curve has to some extent tyrannized the literature on inequality trends.' In a thorough analysis of inequality trends in the UK and the US for the past 300 years, a long enough horizon for the test of any development process, Lindert (1998) finds the Kuznets Curve to be non-existent in these two countries. 'The obsolescence of the Kuznets Curve, in any case, stands out clearly enough in these two countries' recent experience' (Lindert, 1998, p. 29).

Why does the Kuznets Curve fail to exist, at least in a systematic fashion? Most likely because while Kuznets got one force completely right—the higher productivity growth in the urbanizing, industrial areas of a country—he missed out on an equally, if not more powerful, opposing force—the spread of education. In poor countries, labour is a major asset for almost everybody. And educational attainment is a major component of this 'labour asset'. The rich always had education—and more significantly had quality education. The same holds true for the children of the rich. Their educational attainment shows no change over time. In contrast, the bottom 99 per cent increases educational attainment by leaps and bounds.

As part of the development process, after some initial lag, girls begin to enter schools in equal numbers as the boys, and not much later, begin to exceed the educational attainment of boys. Increased education leads to increased labour force participation (LFP), and increased LFP leads to lower fertility, as discussed earlier. This further increases the quality of education of the non-rich, and therefore their absolute and relative earning power. In all of this transition, the rich may have accumulated more physical capital, but have certainly not accumulated *more* quality adjusted labour. This education-led countervailing force is likely to be considerably more than Kuznets' higher productivity growth in the urban areas. Therefore, instead of the inverted-U curve, one should actually expect income distribution to improve with economic growth.

Inequality in the UK, the US, and China

Three countries figure prominently in discussions about inequality change—the UK, the US, and China. A short pen-sketch of inequality trends in each follows. For both the UK and China, the big increase in inequality is likely over.

UK: There has been large-scale inequality change in the UK; the ultimate low was observed in the mid-1970s, when the Gini had gone down to around 30; a trend increase followed till the peak of 49.3 in 2007, and now, after a modest decline has settled at 44.4.

US: A steady pattern has been observed, with the Gini remaining in the high 40s between 1950 and 1994, then moving upward to the present high level of 57.9. Prior to 1993, all households with an income above a million dollars were coded as having income of only a million dollars. Post-1992, the reported incomes of all individuals were coded as actual incomes. This recoding has led to some increase in the observed inequality in the US.

China: Income distribution in China has significantly worsened since the beginning of economic reforms in 1978. From a Gini level of 33.8 in 1980, the 2005 Gini level of income inequality in China was a high 55, i.e., an increase of more than 60 per cent. China has also had high growth, and therefore it is easy to claim that the Kuznets Curve is alive and well, and that high growth 'inevitably' leads to increasing inequality. In absolute and developing country comparative terms, this level of inequality is not that high. Countries in Latin America and Sub-Saharan Africa have inequalities somewhat higher (around 55–65), while in developed economies, the level of inequality is considerably lower. Data subsequent to 2005 does show a marginal decline in inequality to 53.2.

It is a common, near universal phenomenon that measured inequality increases when formerly communist economies move to a 'market' system, for e.g., China, Russia, Vietnam, etc. For many such countries (e.g., Russia), inequality in measured income prior to the change did not reflect 'true' income as embodied in housing, government perks, subsidies on major consumption items, etc.

Measures of inequality and change

The results presented so far do not justify the perceived conventional wisdom that globalization has been bad for inequality, and/or that high growth is invariably accompanied by a large change in inequality. Why this disconnect? One possibility is that the perceptions in the Anglo-Saxon world dominate 'intellectual' and media thinking on the subject.

Pictures speak louder than words. Presented here are three charts of inequality for three regions of the world: the developed economies (AEs plus countries belonging to the former USSR), developing economies, and the world itself. Besides Gini, two other measures of inequality are presented: the ratio of incomes of the top 10 per cent to the bottom 10 per cent (the rich and the poor) and the now popular index of the share of income accruing to the top 1 per cent.

The West (AEs plus countries belonging to the former Soviet Union) and the Rest

No matter what the criteria, and regardless of the talk, income distribution has shown a steep decline since the late 1990s. As discussed above, two prominent members of this group—the UK and the USA (and especially the USA)—have seen sharp increases in inequality. But the weight of this increase has obviously been overshadowed by higher growth in the poorer (not as rich) parts of the West.

Aggregate inequality indices (for large heterogeneous populations) do not change much in percentage terms. While the Gini is down only about 6 per cent from its 'local' peak during 1998–2000, the change is large in historical terms and does represent a reversal.

The much-touted share of the top 1 per cent has stayed constant around 8 per cent for the last two decades. The ratio of the share of the very rich (top 10 per cent) and the very poor (bottom 10 per cent) parallels the move in the Gini. *Thus, all three indices point to improving inequality in the Western world.* So I repeat my question. Whose inequality and why the angst?

FIGURE 9.1: TRENDS IN INCOME DISTRIBUTION—THE WEST

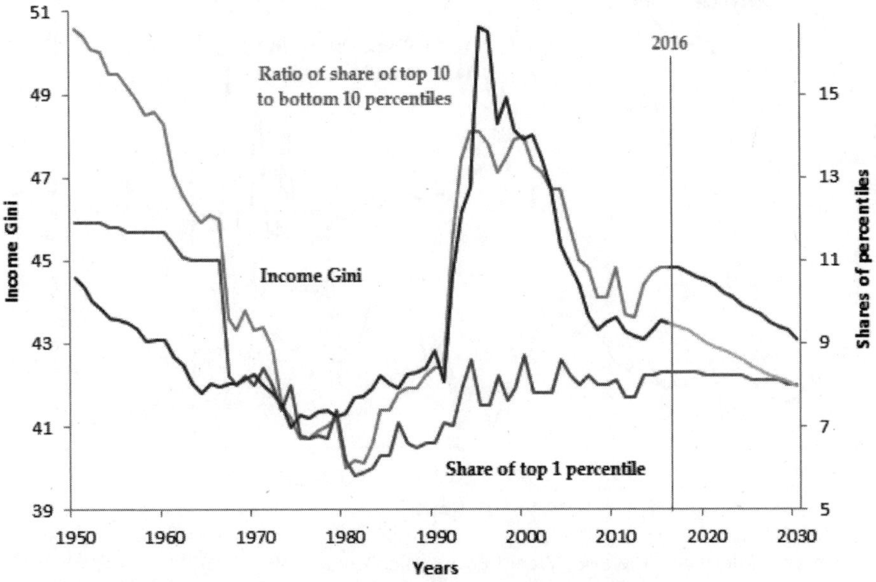

Source: Piketty WID.world; World Economic Outlook, IMF (2017); author computations.

Notes: The West is inclusive of the erstwhile Soviet Union. All indicators 2017 onwards are extrapolations.

FIGURE 9.2: TRENDS IN INCOME DISTRIBUTION—DEVELOPING ECONOMIES

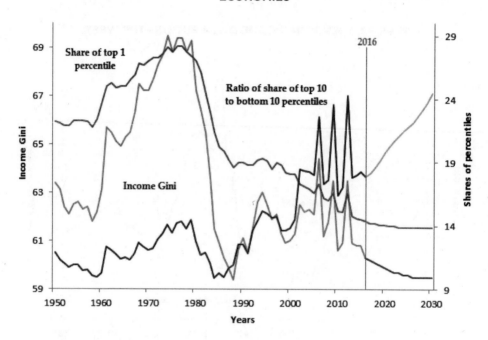

Source: Piketty WID.world; World Economic Outlook, IMF (2017); author computations.

Note: Developing countries are countries outside of the AEs and the former Soviet Union.
All indicators 2017 onwards are extrapolations.

FIGURE 9.3: TRENDS IN INCOME DISTRIBUTION—WORLD

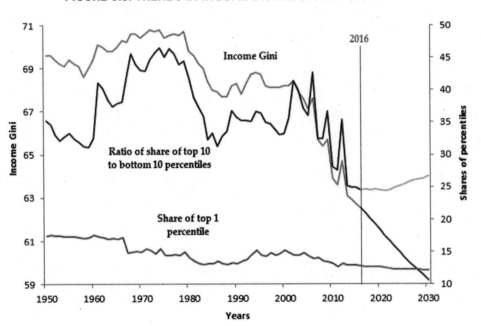

Source: Piketty WID.world; World Economic Outlook, IMF (2017); author computations.

Note: All indicators 2017 onwards are extrapolations.

10

Poverty is Old, Basic Income is New

Don't stop thinking about tomorrow
Don't stop, it'll soon be here
It'll be here better than before
Yesterday's gone, yesterday's gone

—Don't Stop *by* Fleetwood Mac
(*lyrics by* Christine McVie, Rumours, 1977)

Poverty and the distribution of income are two subjects that have been studied for centuries. In the mid-19th century, when Engels and Marx wrote their Manifesto, a document that was to be a rallying cry for the downtrodden for the next 100 years, about 60 per cent of the UK population was absolutely poor according to the dollar-a-day line. In the developing economies, the proportion was close to 90 per cent—life in the developing world was truly poor, brutish and short.

The decline in world poverty in the last forty years is truly one of the great miracles of history; strike that, it *is* the greatest miracle. It was some fifty-five years ago that policy discussion about removing poverty became part of a government document (Planning Commission, 1962). Soon after, President Lyndon Johnson sounded the first bugle in the War on Poverty in an advanced economy, the US. A few years later, former US Secretary of Defense Robert McNamara started his leadership tenure at the World Bank, committing that organization to the removal of world poverty. In 1980, the world was counting calories, in the mistaken belief that caloric intake was an indication of dire, absolute poverty straits. Not many believed then, perhaps even today, that caloric intake would go the way of cholesterol or vice versa.

Giving the World Bank its due, which is rare for ex-staffers like me, the fact remains that the organization was at the cutting edge of thinking and research on absolute poverty. Caloric intake was a misstep, but such detours are necessary in the path of research. The developing world was poor, at a high level, until about 2000. In 1990, the World Bank offered the first absolute poverty line—the one PPP $ per person per day. This codification was announced in the World Development Report—a flagship publication of the World Bank. Going by this metric, 57 per cent of the developing world was poor in 1990. Poverty had declined since 1870, when the dollar-a-day poor were estimated to have numbered about 87 per cent of the developing world's population. In 1970, the fraction was 73 per cent; in 1990, 57 per cent. But it all happened so fast!

The developing world was truly poor in the 1870s, and in the 1980s. Within twelve years of origination, the dollar-a-day poverty line was going to become obsolete, a subject matter I dealt with, at some length, in my book *Imagine There's No Country*. The book documents that the esteemed World Bank, and/or its scholars, were not being fair to the 'truth' when they claimed that removal of absolute poverty remained a big challenge. Also questionable was the World Bank's claim that not much had been done to remove poverty, and all that the world needed was just fractionally more aid from the rich countries which would go a mile, and further, to ameliorate the misery of the poor.

The poverty industry was born when, predictably, poverty was falling the fastest. There were high-paid jobs to be protected, as well as a do-gooder place in history. The international organizations went to extraordinary lengths to keep the myth going. I know from personal experience because the Asian Development Bank (ADB) had commissioned me to do an eighteen-country poverty study, with the active involvement of the statisticians from these countries. I completed the study, called 'Asian Drama Revisited', and came to the conclusion that Asian poverty circa 2000 was not a billion-plus

(ADB party line) but closer to half that magnitude. Now 500–600 million is a very, very large number of absolute poor; the dream that this number should be zero is the dream of everyone, not just well-paid staffers paid to keep the dream alive.

However, the project work was not published by the ADB. Readers can check out the entire document at www.ssbhalla. org, and figure out if there is any valid reason for this. Just look around you, and tell me that absolute poverty has not declined substantially in just the last fifteen years. You can't fight Mother Nature. And you shouldn't either, because you are bound to lose, like the povertarians[46] of yesteryear.

As a recount of the signposts on absolute poverty, we must remember that China and India were dirt poor in the 1970s. Many, including Nobel laureate Gunnar Myrdal, had given these two population and poverty giants up for dead a decade earlier. Aid (remember foreign aid?) was considered the perfect antidote to poverty removal, and Millennium Development Goals were set to reduce absolute poverty by half by 2015.

Twenty-five years after the inaugural *World Development Report 1990: Poverty* of the World Bank, the talk has moved on to the emerging middle class[47] and the middle class. Absolute poverty has been reduced to a Sub-Saharan Africa problem—still mega, still of major concern, but instead of 2.5 billion people twenty-five years ago, it is *only* about 400 million today.

What really happened, and why so fast? For starters, education, again. Not that the provision of education and health were not considered essential for the removal of poverty and for the prospect of well-being before. Under the guidance of Nobel laureate Amartya Sen and Mahbub ul Haq, the UN offered an alternative to the rankings of countries—the Human Development Index (HDI).

The noteworthy feature about this index was that it offered to measure education and health as *non-monetary* indices of well-being. This emphasis on the non-monetary aspect of education is one reason why the HDI index of welfare missed out on the transformation of China and India. As the reader by now must be well aware, I regard education as the most transformative force in human history. The acquisition of education is the road to welfare. The HDI index was offered as an *alternative* to welfare levels as revealed by GDP per capita (the I in HDI refers to income); it should have been offered as the leading indicator of future growth, as documented in the next chapter. The difference is that the old elite sees education as an end in itself and only loosely connected to monetary welfare or poverty reduction.

Counting the poor

The World Bank (as well as other international organizations) has spent considerable amounts of money trying to identify the absolute poor. Many researchers (including me) have done a lot of research into the minutiae of poverty measurement. But the education data assembled by Barro-Lee suggests that there is a real shortcut to the *measurement* of the incidence of absolute poverty. Just measure the fraction of illiterates in the age group of fifteen to sixty-four years in the world, and multiply that fraction by 0.83,[48] and you will have a very good estimate of absolute poverty.

This 'achievement' should not be underestimated. Volumes of books have been written on poverty, and many of them involving India, and the endless debate in India on how to accurately measure absolute poverty. (In India, we also debate whether gravity is actually 32 ft/sec^2). There are involved comparisons with poverty in China, and how much poverty in India is above that of China (actually, not much, as shown below). Like all good research, only 'repetitive' analysis can isolate *true* facts, especially for subjects as emotive as inequality and poverty.

FIGURE 10.1: WORLD ILLITERACY AND WORLD ABSOLUTE POVERTY: CAUSE AND EFFECT

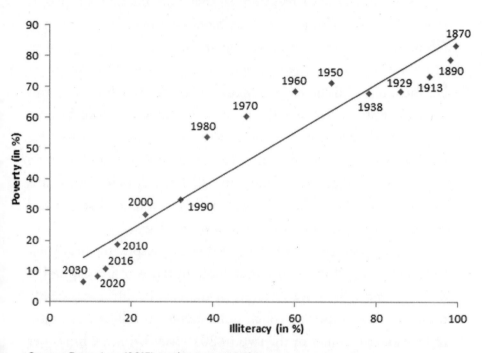

Source: Barro-Lee (2015); author computations.

Note: The definition of absolute poverty is given by the World Bank ($1.9/day in 2011 PPP prices). All indicators 2017 onwards are extrapolations.

Figure 10.1 is quite emphatic about the role of education in alleviating poverty. Whether it is 1870 that one is talking about or 2016, the prediction of the simple model (percentage poor in the developing world being explained by percentage illiterate) is more than reasonably accurate (for the statistically inclined, an R^2 of 0.96). In 1870, the poor in the world were more than 80 per cent;

the predicted poor (along the line of fit; depicted in figure), 90 per cent. Almost 150 years later, the actual poor are at 12 per cent while the predicted poor are at 17 per cent.

Absolute poverty in India and China: Nearly the same

The near universal perception is that the fraction of people absolutely poor in India is not only higher but much higher than in China. Two reasons have been offered. First (and this is a problem of definition), a non-poor person saving a reasonable fraction of her income is considered poor because poverty is defined in terms of consumption. Second, the poor in China are not allowed to migrate with as much freedom as the poor in India. Visitors see the beggars in the streets of the major cities of India and form an impression; if migration of the poor is curtailed, as in China, this vision can be distorted. And then, there is a more important third reason—mismeasurement arising out of the data.

An unappreciated fact to be noted is that despite the nearly 4:1 advantage that China enjoys over India in terms of per capita US dollar income, the poverty levels in the two countries are nearly the same. This surprising conclusion emerges as follows. The ratio of US dollar incomes of the two in 2016 was 3.7, i.e., China's per capita income was 3.7 times that of India's per capita income. However, the World Bank definition of absolute poverty is in terms of PPP consumption in 2011 prices (poverty defined to be less than US $1.9 per day in terms of consumption as estimated by household surveys). The per capita PPP income ratio in the two economies in 2016 was 2.1; still no reason to believe that poverty in the two economies should be near equal.

Now, the poverty matter begins to get complicated. Household consumption in India is 64 per cent of household income; in

China, the corresponding ratio is a low 44.1 per cent, one of the lowest in the non-oil world. Some (including myself) believe that poverty should be defined in terms of income, not consumption. But the World Bank, the final arbiter on poverty measurement, believes it should be defined in terms of consumption. Given the above consumption ratios in the two economies (44 per cent and 64 per cent), the PPP per capita income advantage in China is further reduced from 2.1 to 1.4.

But there is an additional adjustment: the consumption *distribution* in the two economies is not equal. The bottom 20 per cent of the population consumes 4.7 per cent share in China, and an 8.1 per cent share in India, i.e., the consumption distribution in India is more equal than China. This share differential among the bottom 20 per cent means that the average consumption ratio in the two economies is now 0.81, i.e., the bottom 20 per cent Chinese now has a lower consumption level than the bottom 20 per cent Indian. If stated somewhat differently, perhaps even shockingly, absolute poverty grips a higher proportion of the population in China than in India.

That doesn't seem so right, does it? Because according to the World Bank data in 2011 prices, there were close to 9 per cent absolute poor in China, compared to 22 per cent such poor in India. This is 'correct' because the World Bank measures poverty in terms of the estimate as revealed by household surveys. And household surveys in China attribute more than 80 per cent of measured national accounts consumption to households; in India, in 2011–2012, less than 50 per cent of measured national accounts consumption is attributed to households. With this correction, the average consumption advantage is back in favour of China— the 0.81 ratio now becomes 1.3 (0.81*80/50), i.e., the average consumption of the bottom 20 per cent in China is 30 per cent higher than in India

There is a final twist. It is that until the 2011–2012 survey, food consumption in India was based on a thirty day recall period, while, as Nobel laureate Deaton and others have argued, food consumption is more accurately measured on a seven day recall basis. In 2011–2012, two parallel consumption surveys were undertaken in India. One survey followed the traditional thirty day measurement guidelines, while the other measured food on a seven day basis. The result: a decline in measured absolute poverty from 24 per cent of the population to 12 per cent. That is just 4 percentage points higher than absolute poverty in China, and probably is a correct reflector of the underlying reality.

Basic Income: An idea whose time was yesterday and tomorrow

Poverty in most economies (outside of Sub-Saharan Africa) is in single digits, and declining. It is unlikely that any major institution in the world (e.g., World Bank, IMF) will be talking any more about the need to alleviate absolute poverty. Inequality discussions are also likely to become passé. What is very likely to become centre-stage, and with equal applicability in both developed and developing economies, is the new curse of progress—large-scale unemployment or minimal employment.

The old source of jobs—industrialization—has been continually declining in its potency.[49] Several new-era services, for e.g., banking, require a lot fewer workers. The number of those educated, even college-educated, is rapidly increasing. But the demand for 'traditional' jobs is declining. It is going to be a brave new world, with brave new problems.

There is one possible solution, at least a partial one, to the emerging social tensions. It is the provision of a minimum income for all, the much talked about 'universal basic income' or UBI. The essence of UBI is that societies can now afford to provide a minimum income to *all* the citizens. Each individual can supplement her income by working, but if she is not able to work, no problem, she is assured of a minimum level of income.

Seems like a great idea, so what is wrong with UBI? That it was tried before and failed miserably. Each generation is entitled to its own mistakes, but each generation of thinkers or policymakers also believes they are Newtonesque. In a 1944 book, *The Great Transformation,* Karl Polanyi documents what happened in Speenhamland, England in 1795.

There is no social scientist who has not concluded that the market system does not yield the optimal or most socially desirable distribution of income. England had a free labour market prior to 1795. However, Polanyi writes that 'the economic advantages of a free labour market could not make up for the social destruction wrought by it. Regulation of a new type had to be introduced under which labour was again protected, only this time from the working of the market mechanism itself.'

In other words, workers were not even paid a minimum 'survival' income. Hence:

The justices of Berkshire, meeting at the Pelikan Inn, in Speenhamland, near Newbury, on May 6, 1795, in a time of great distress, decided that subsidies in aid of wages should be granted in accordance with a scale dependent upon the price of bread, so that a minimum income should be assured to the poor *irrespective of their earnings* (author's emphasis added in italics).

This guarantee of a minimum income proved the undoing of the system. Each person was guaranteed the same level of income; the only day-to-day change was in the amount to be given to each person. This amount varied with the price of bread, but not with the poverty of the recipient, i.e., each person ended up with the same level of income, whether they worked or not. So nobody worked, and the scheme failed.

Moral of the story: incentives work. In the mid-1950s, Milton Friedman came up with the idea of a negative income tax. Under his system, the payments will be on a graduated scale, and the recipient will have a higher take-home income the more she works.

Given the worldwide declining trend of job creation, societies will have to be creative in designing new welfare systems. Those that exist were for the old world order, a world with deep education and income inequalities. Education inequality has declined, and will continue to decline. However, social tensions are likely to rise, with jobs not available relative to aspirations and education investments. Negative income tax for those in the labour force can be one policy. In addition, technology now allows for the identification of the poor not in the labour force—targeting these individuals will now be easier. With these two policies, the Speenhamland mistake can easily be avoided.

11

Education: The Driver of the Middle Class

Padhoge likhoge toh banoge nawab
Jo tum kheloge kudoge toh hoge kharab

—Old Indian Limerick

This limerick opening this chapter, loosely translated, goes something like this: 'If you study, read, and write, you will become a nawab; if you go and jump and play, you will become bad.' Now, the word 'nawab' does not quite rhyme with bad, but the Hindi word for bad (kharab), does rhyme with nawab. I remember this from my school days in the 1950s which means that the belief in education providing a springboard for upward mobility and becoming middle class was alive, and well, in the streets of Kirkee, a town near Pune, India. Actually, 'nawab' means a prince, but none of us believed that we would become royalty via education. But we did believe that via studies, we would have riches, like a prince. Substitute 'Tiger Mom' lyrics (if available) for the limerick, and I am sure the content will be the same.

When I was singing the 'be-educated' and 'be-middle-class' songs, less than 1 per cent of Indians had attended college, and less than 1 per cent of Indians were middle class. Today, about 15 per cent have attended college, in the age group of fifteen to sixty-four, and 46 per cent are middle class. But by juxtaposing the two, we are getting ahead of the story. Let us backtrack, and attempt to define the middle class.

The middle class is a much talked about subject at cocktail parties and academic discourses. Everyone not only has an opinion on it, but a strong opinion. However, what really is this mythical being called the middle class?

By its very name, the middle class is often treated as the middle of the population. Indeed, popular academic discourses on the middle class define it to be the second, third, and fourth quintiles of the population ranked by per capita income, with the two tails (the bottom and top quintiles) bringing up the edges. This middle of the distribution, like the poor, is always with us, and always approximately the same percentage of the population. However, this middle is unlikely to be the middle class as either historically defined or understood.

FIGURE 11.1: COLLEGE EDUCATION AND THE MIDDLE CLASS—CAUSE AND EFFECT?

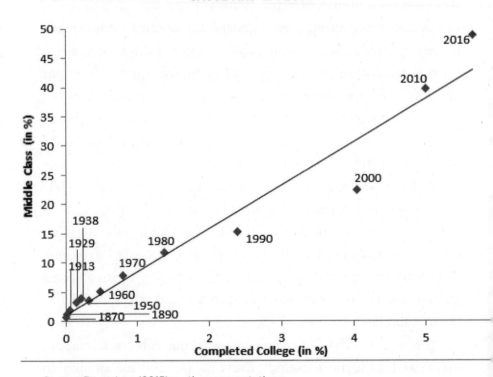

Source: Barro-Lee (2015); author computations.

Note: Definition of the middle class—between $12 PPP per person per day and $120 a day in 2011 PPP prices.

Historically, from Aristotle to Barrington Moore, the middle class was often a very small fraction of the population; for long periods, it comprised less than a tenth, if not less than a twentieth, of the total population. That was before the expansion of education, or less than two hundred years ago.

Figure 11.1 documents the simplest of relationships—the fraction of the population that is middle class (as defined later in the chapter) and the fraction that has a college degree. The education data is from Barro-Lee (2015), i.e., the data on the fraction of population that has obtained a college degree, and the data is available since 1870. No adjustment has been made for the quality of the college education or the grade obtained.

The y-axis represents the fraction of the population, estimated by us, that can be defined as middle class. Let us ponder over the chart for just a bit longer. Each 1 per cent expansion in college degree completion in the developing countries leads to an additional 4.2 per cent joining the middle class. This relationship held true in 1870 and holds true even today.

The two data series could not be more different in their construction, yet there is a close relationship. College completion data is just a counting of individuals obtaining a college degree. It is painstaking work (we have Barro-Lee to thank), and I don't want in any way to understate its importance, and especially, its importance for this book.[50] The construction of the middle class data is an equally painstaking job, but the process is somewhat more 'questionable' or 'debatable'. If it is based on income (which it is), then one must ask the question: what is the definition of income? And if it is real income, then what is the definition of the price series? These questions are all addressed in this chapter, but I want to emphasize that the construction of the middle class line is 'arbitrary', and hence to observe such a close relationship, is, well, beautiful. There is an intuitive connection between the two, a connection that was not apparent to me when I waxed eloquent about defining the middle class in an earlier attempt way back in 2007 (*Second among Equals*).

Middle class: Historical definitions

Obviously, one definition is that you are middle class if you have obtained a college degree. But that is a bit after the fact, and what happens when everyone has a college degree? And how do you then graduate from the middle class to the rich?

In popular discourse, and following from definitions, there are only three income classes in the world—the poor, the rich, and those in between, the middle. The class here is defined in income ranges, but as sociologists have continually reminded us, class is much more than just income. In other words, a person can acquire wealth and be rich, and yet not have 'class'. Note that of the three income ranges only one has the word 'class' as its main theme.

Educational achievement also has three strata—primary, secondary, and tertiary. But there is also a fourth category: those who do not have any education, i.e., the 'illiterates'. In *Second among Equals*, little attempt was made to formally integrate education distribution with that of income, but it did emphasize that the middle class was a class apart. How much apart is provided by references to philosophers, and historians, and political scientists.

The middle class is not the middle of the distribution, but rather a set of values and virtues, whose acquisition almost requires at least upper secondary and college education. Aristotle and John Stuart Mill were early champions of the middle class. The middle class got bad press when the Communist Manifesto confused it with whatever was felt to be bad and transitory—feudalism, imperialism, fascism, and communism. It was left to Barrington Moore to revive and justifiably credit the middle class with several liberal and progressive forces in history.

Some have defined the middle to be the middle tendency in terms of values or opinions. For e.g., a middle of the road opinion or someone between the left and right, whether a liberal or a conservative. Middle class is also assumed to be the same as the middle tendency. For e.g., in the US, the diehard Republicans are the rich elite; the dyed-in-the-wool Democrats represent the poor. So the middle class represents those who are neither rich nor poor, neither Republican nor Democrat.

Defining the middle class—From Aristotle to Marx

This might be the modern definition of the middle class, but historically, a particular kind of elite has been defined as the middle class. For Aristotle, the middle class owned property. As quoted in Anesi (2003):

> Private property is abolished in the Republic, but in a polity Aristotle views it as necessity. 'Property must also belong to [the citizens], for the citizens must have a supply of property . . . land should belong to those who bear arms and to those who share in the constitution.' Aristotle claims that the middle class will not be able to rule unless they are essentially given a push up, and that push is *property ownership*; *private property* enables the middle class to rule. 'Since it is admitted that moderation and the mean are always best it is clear that in the ownership of all gifts of fortune a middle condition will be the best' (emphasis added).

It is difficult to obtain an explicit Marxian definition of the middle class. At various points in the Communist Manifesto, this is how it is defined (or left ambiguous):

The bourgeoisie has stripped of its halo every occupation hitherto honored and looked up to with reverent awe. It has converted the physician, the lawyer, the priest, the poet, the man of science, into its paid wage labourers.

So one knows who the middle class is *not*. It is also not:

[...] the lower middle class, the small manufacturer, the shopkeeper, the artisan, the peasant, all these fight against the bourgeoisie, to save from extinction their existence as fractions of the middle class.

But there are clues.

The middle class theory by the communists may be summed up in a single sentence: 'Abolition of private property.' And finally, to quote something explicit: 'By freedom is meant, under the present bourgeois conditions of production, free trade, free selling and buying. You must, therefore, confess that by "individual" you mean no other person than the bourgeois, than the *middle-class owner of property*. This person must, indeed, be swept out of the way, and made impossible' (emphasis added). So, according to Engels and Marx, the bourgeoisie middle class was really the property owning elite, i.e., the same as Aristotle.

Aristotle was brought up as a technocrat aristocrat. His father was a professional (physician), so it is likely that Aristotle was reflecting, via the middle class, his own family background. As was John Stuart Mill, by the way, more than two thousand years later. Mill had a similar definition of the middle class. He also had a near identical upbringing; he was brought up as an aristocrat, with his father a major philosopher (John Mill) and his godfather Jeremy Bentham. Again, his visualization of the middle class encompassed the elite (like himself and like Aristotle):

Mill defines the middle class also by amount rather than source of income. The middle class consists of persons with moderate income or property ... Mill places so much emphasis upon class and upon changes in class structure because he assumes that ideology follows from class position. He assumes that the middle class participates in public discussions, attends to good leaders, and comes to understand its situation and its interests. (Sullivan, 1981)

Barrington Moore, on his part, agrees with Marx:

We may simply register strong agreement with the Marxist thesis that a vigorous and independent class of town dwellers has been an indispensable element in the growth of parliamentary democracy. No bourgeois, no democracy (p. 418).

In his book on the middle class in Great Britain, Lawrence James concludes similarly:

As entrepreneurs and manufacturers, the middle class created modern, urban Britain, and on the whole [the] central government was happy to let them mould its environment. In what was some of the most influential and far-reaching legislation ever passed, Westminster delegated extensive powers to elected councils. These were dominated by a middle class with a compelling faith in its own capacity to make the world a cleaner, healthier, more secure *and better-educated place*. It started with the urban infrastructure, laying drains, purifying water and paving and lighting streets. Then it turned its attentions to civic amenities such as baths, libraries, parks, museums and the supply of gas and electricity. These often massive programmes of regeneration and modernization enhanced the middle class's image of Britain as a progressive and civilized nation (p.232, emphasis added).

Middle class—Measurement

The subject of the middle class was first explored in some detail in a May 2007 manuscript prepared by me for the Peterson Institute for International Economics. The name of the manuscript—*Second among Equals: The Middle Class Kingdoms of India and China*. Its subject—the definition of the middle class, its evolution, and spread, and forecasts. Today, exactly a decade later and with additional data, we are completing the project by filling in one of the major gaps in SAE—the income definition, while correct, did *not* have a sociological or economic explanation; we *now* have an *education* explanation for the different income classes, and especially the middle class.

The definition of the middle class offered in SAE was simple and straightforward, and has been repeated for this book. The search was for a definition that would pass the test of time, space, and common sense. It should hold true for several hundred years ago, hold true today, and tomorrow (say, in another hundred years). It should conform to our sense of three classes—the poor, the middle, and the rich. To define three classes, one needs to define two lines—the line dividing the poor and the middle class, and the line dividing the middle class and the rich.

Depending on where you were with reference to Paul Simon—'One man's ceiling is another man's floor'—if you crossed the line, you were no longer poor. The next question which arises is: how do you define the poor? Again, this is a question which needs an answer that cuts across time and space, and with more objectivity and less subjectivity. Modern nation states, from poor countries like India to a rich country like the US, have attempted to define their respective poverty lines. The poverty–middle class line should be one that is commonly accepted among the rich countries of the world. There is no higher absolute level of poverty income than that obtained in the advanced economies. This explains the productive search in 2005 (in SAE) to obtain the poverty lines, in local currencies, for the rich countries of the world.

These individual country poverty lines were converted into a common currency, the 1996 PPP series. As luck would have it, the population-weighted PPP poverty line in 2006 was PPP $10 per person per day. An appealing number, and hence, the proliferation, and acceptance of US $10 as *the* middle class line by international institutions (Asian Development Bank) and researchers (Homi Kharas).[51] Bhalla–Kharas, in their work on Malaysia, came across a particular research shortcoming: 'Though considerable research has been undertaken on pinpointing the poverty line, relatively little attention has been concerned on defining the demarcation line for the rich, and for the middle class' (1991, p. 26). They then proceeded to provide such a definition, and indeed provided explicit levels for the beginning of the lower middle class, upper middle class, etc.

The middle class is defined for all peoples, in a common PPP currency, no matter where they reside. By extension, this definition of the middle class extends across time, in the future as well as in the past.

There is now a new 2011-based PPP price series. According to this data (again, conversion of local currency into a common currency) the poverty–middle class line is revealed to be PPP $12 per person per day. Once a middle class definition is obtained, the beginning of the rich class should be a straightforward matter. It is the case, but the definition is also arbitrary. There are no accepted definitions of the rich, though a reasonable starting point (and one used here) is that the *beginning level for the rich is ten times the starting level of the middle class.* Hence, PPP $120 and above defines the rich (in 2006 prices, this had the added convenience and attraction of being PPP $100 per person per day). Note that these are the same levels in US dollar prices since one US dollar, by definition, is equal to one PPP dollar at any point of time.

Historical support for the modern definition of the middle class

In 1850, only 3 per cent of the world's population was middle class. In his detailed study on the middle class in Great Britain in the middle of the 19th century, James (2006) concludes that an earning level of £146 a year identified the beginning of the middle class. This level was also the beginning of the taxable bracket in England, a finding found for China and India more than 150 years later.

Converting a family income level of £146 a year to present US dollar prices yields the result that our middle class definition is very close to James' definition. The £–$ exchange rate was 0.2 in 1850; hence, £146 a year in 1850 was worth US $730 a year. The US price level in 1850 was 3.62; in 2011, it was 100. Hence, US $730 then translates into US $20165 (730*100/3.62) a year or US $55 a day. If a one-earner family was the norm in 1850, then US $55 a day for a family of five translates into US $11 per person per day circa 2011. That is awfully close to our US $12 (or PPP $12) a day definition. Given this historical support from James' thorough study for England in 1850, and the relationship of this definition with college completion over the last 150 years, *we declare the case and debate closed over the definition of the middle class line. It is the poverty line in advanced economies.* End of story.

Middle class, economic reforms, and growth

The middle class, as defined by Aristotle and/or John Stuart Mill, starts off as the technocratic elite, but once its ranks swell it begins to exercise its influence. This middle class is interested in a levelling of the playing field. Through reforms and sensible policies, the middle class is able to affect future growth.

The middle class is neither the aristocracy (landed or otherwise) nor feudal. The middle class represents the polity that has benefitted the most from economic growth; hence, as part of their class interests, the middle class is very desirous of economic reforms, and is often in a position to ensure its perpetuation. The middle class is a class that believes in education and merit. Indeed, a belief in merit may be the middle class' signature.

In the early stages of development, the rich are the landed elite; also, in the early stages, some of the landed elite venture into industry, and some become industrial entrepreneurs. As is well understood by all, this landed industrial elite is interested in its own gains, and therefore believes in high protection, low economic freedom, etc. They are the 'rent-seekers', and it is logical for them to want to stay that way. They are the anti-reformers.

By definition, the middle class is neither the poor nor the rich. The middle class is a sense of values, an indicator of aspirations, a belief in 'law and order'. In contrast to the landed industrial elite, the middle class comprises individuals who made money the old-fashioned way—by earning it. Thus, it is logical for the middle class to believe in the opposite of what the traditional elite believes. Its own self-interest demands an increase in its own welfare, but its gains can come only from a more open economy, from less control on its own enterprise, from greater economic freedom. Thus, the middle class and the traditional elites demand opposite 'rules' of behaviour, opposite institutions. In this battle, the middle class has to win out—due to its sheer size, if not the logic of its position. This is why 'good' institutions and development are inevitable. Institutional development is the development of the middle class. This is true in Aristotle's Greece, in Mill's England, and today in India and China, and in the rest of the poorer developing world tomorrow.

There are numerous instances in history (South Korea in the 1970s, Chile in the 1970s and 1980s, China in the 1990s and today) when the middle class has shied away from demanding what it believes in the political sphere. For it, merit-based economic growth, which enhances its own relative value, is at a lexicographic premium to everything else. And merit can only be enhanced by increases in both the quantity, and especially the quality, of education. But extra education is no good in a feudal, closed economy. Therefore, the middle class is at the forefront of education, *and in demands for opening up the economy*. So economic freedom, in all its manifestations, is the second demand of the middle class. After such demands are near fully met, the middle class turns its considerable clout and attention to demanding improvements in the political institutions landscape. It is the rise of the middle class which very likely gives rise to institutions; hence, institutional development is likely within the growth process (endogenous), rather than affecting it from the outside, i.e., exogenous.

Education, the middle class, and globalization

Education, the middle class, and globalization—three near synonymous words, all pointing, and correctly so, to the expansion of the middle class and growth in developing economies. There is a strong suggestion that it is the acquisition of education that brings about an increase in income, which brings about an entry into the middle class. There is also a strong suggestion that the values of the middle class are formed not by the increase in income, but by the education which propels the increase in income. The guiding spirit behind the 'technocratic elite'—the reform orientation, the obsession with merit—are all aspects of the middle class brought about by the pursuit of education.

If education is the driving force, then economic growth should be associated with the acquisition of education. One challenge for economists has been to identify, *ex-ante*, the reasons for growth successes or growth takeoffs. The data presented below is one such attempt. While the middle class proportion does vary considerably among the successes at the start of their success, the average years of schooling is robustly 'fixed' around four years.

Table 11.1 documents some data on growth takeoffs in a number of developing economies. The growth takeoff is defined to be a sustained 6 per cent growth level for at least a decade. The definition of takeoff is such as to broadly define a growth acceleration, a break in the growth series, if you will. Hong Kong was the first developing economy to experience a growth acceleration in 1962; India was the last developing economy to do so in 1994. The list is not meant to be exhaustive, just illustrative. With the exception of Chile and Sri Lanka, most growth takeoffs seem to occur when the average educational level in the adult working population is around four years.

China experienced a growth takeoff with an average educational level of 5.9 years. This hints at a delay brought about by communist experiments. Its middle class level, at the time of the structural break in growth, was only 0.7 per cent of the population—by far the lowest among the countries reported in the table. Correspondingly,

TABLE 11.1: GROWTH TAKEOFFS, EDUCATION, AND THE MIDDLE CLASS

Country	Year	Average Years of Schooling	Middle Class	Secondary or College Completion	Per Capita Income
			as % of total population		(in 2011 PPP)
Hong Kong	1962	5.4	27.9	14.0	4899
South Korea	1963	5.2	2.6	12.6	1539
Taiwan	1963	4.0	8.2	12.6	2717
Thailand	1966	2.5	6.3	2.4	1864
Singapore	1966		40.3		5829
Indonesia	1968	2.7	3.1	1.9	1454
Brazil	1968	3.1	7.6	5.8	3158
Malaysia	1971	4.5	27.3	8.6	4136
Chile	1977	6.9	33.9	18.5	5703
China	1982	5.9	0.7	14.6	1085
Sri Lanka	1993	9.5	18.8	47.2	3501
Vietnam	1993		2.6		1554
India	1994	4.2	5.9	9.0	1898

Source: Barro-Lee (2015); IMF WEO Database (April 2017): author computations.
Note: 'Year' represents the beginning year of growthacceleration, with growth level post-acceleration defined as being above 6 per cent per annum.

the per capita income level is also the lowest—just PPP $1100. It is crucial to note here that India started its reform-induced growth journey with a per capita income level almost twice that of China.

This brings us to the final 'relationship', the modern day chicken and egg question: does globalization bring about the acquisition of education, or does education result in greater globalization?

Globalization does induce greater trade, more travel, and faster dissemination of new ideas. It allows for the faster spread of technology into new products. But it is knowledge that allows technology to develop, and knowledge for innovation can only come about from education. Further, as the opening limerick showed, income at the end of education is what drives most individuals. Education is the springboard for faster and more efficient globalization. Case closed.

12

Education and the Democratization of the Elite

Come on, people now
Smile on your brother
Everybody get together
Try to love one another right now

—Get Together *by* The Youngbloods
(*lyrics by* Chet Powers)

Change brings about further change; profound changes tend to have larger effects than shallow ones. We have noted the sharp non-linear change that has occurred in most developing countries since 1980—the most profound change being in China. But that is in per capita income and income growth. In terms of education, even more dramatic changes have taken place in the developing world since the mid-1990s—and especially in the segment of youth education, in the age group of fifteen to twenty-four. Thus, for many of these economies, there has been a vast increase in the share of the voting age population that is educated; for e.g., in developing countries, the mean education level of the youth (fifteen to twenty-four years) increased from 5.7 years in 1980 to 6.4 years in 1990 and to 9.5 years in 2015. In that same year, the comparable number for the developed world was 11.8 years, i.e., a small gap of only 2.3 years. Back in 1980, this gap was four years.

The educated became richer—aka less poor—and eventually more middle class. The more educated you are, the more likely you are to be democratic. And if a nation is already a democracy (like India), the more likely it is that the numerous entrants into the educated (above high school) level will make their presence felt in their choice of political leaders as well as policies. Only 7 per cent of the population aged fifteen to sixty-four years had attended college in developing economies in 1991; in 2014, the proportion had more than doubled to 14+ per cent.

What we know from historical data is that the larger the middle class and the more educated the population, the stronger a democracy is. But 'the more educated' also means a considerable fraction of the educated elite is now composed of new, first-time entrants—first-generation members coming from the never-before middle class segments—in many ways, an entirely new elite. And when that happens, it is a mega unique event, and something most developing economy societies have never experienced before. Hence, there is a lot of social churn and social change. The issue is not for better or for worse; the reality is that we should not be surprised that large discrete changes in educational attainment lead to changes in the composition of the elite—and that these changes are in opposition to the old elite.

But elites, if I may say, have the survival ability of a cockroach— you can go from nobility to feudalism, and there is very little change in the ruling top. From feudalism you proceed to capitalism, and by and large, the old feudals become the new robber barons. From capitalism you proceed towards communism, and the elites are the same. From communism you drive upward to Fabian socialism, and you guessed it right, the new elites continue to be indistinguishable from the old elites. The more things change, the more they remain the same—clichés are clichés because they have a ring of truth in them.

But what happens when the composition of the elite changes? What happens when the elites are much more numerous, and drawn from a larger democratic pot? What happens when in the top 20 per cent of the society, every individual has attained the same high level of education, and therefore, theoretically, has the same earning power? That is when you can have the *possibility* of a revolution.

In the previous chapter, we had talked about the large changes observed in the size of the middle class in the world. There is very little difference between the middle class and the elite. The elite is broadly composed of professionals, barring the 'few' aristocrats and the hereditary rich. Before the Industrial Revolution, the elites were composed of royalty (religious and otherwise) and their technocratic helpers. With the Industrial Revolution came an expansion of the middle class as well as the elite. However, the correlation between the new and the old was strong—hence the preoccupation of many that inequality just perpetuated itself, or worse, 'the rich got richer and the poor got poorer'.

With education, the old order changed, and changed in a hugely democratic fashion. Suddenly the bottom 99 per cent, and most certainly the bottom 95 per cent, had access to all the goodies so far enjoyed by the exclusive few. This meant that there was a *possibility* of change in the power structure. Note the emphasis on possibility—not a certainty, or even a likelihood, just a possibility.

When the possibility becomes a probability, and the probability a reality, then we observe a change in the elites, and a change forever in the structure of rulers. There is then no turning back to the halcyon, or otherwise, days of the past. Then it becomes a new order.

There are consequences to this huge educational transformation—among them, the increase in people's wealth that has been documented in this book. The fact remains that the mammoth change in education is the most democratic of all the transformations we will ever see—and that too in such a short period of just fifty years. This applies mostly to the developing world, but also to parts of the developed world. Blacks and Asian elites today form a much larger fraction of the elite business and power structure in the US than just twenty years earlier.

The future of traditional elites in a more educated world

It is useful to study the pattern and consequences of the changing of the elites in one large developing economy—India. It is very likely to also be the pattern in other developing economies in the future. India is a leading elite change indicator deserving special attention.

At the time of independence, the average educational achievement of an Indian adult was as low as just one year of schooling. Today, average school attainment is 7.5 years. Moreover, for an Indian youth (between fifteen and twenty-four years) the average attainment level is now more than nine years. In the US, in 2016, the average educational attainment of the youth was 12.1 years. The Indians are catching up quite quickly.

The relevance of these figures is to emphasize the importance of the simple fact that with education enhancement—combined with rapid strides in communication technology—there is simply no place to hide for the traditional elite any more. People have alternative sources of information, and they can judge themselves, instead of being told what to think by old elites.

Previously, the elite in India (and the former colonies of Great Britain) were identified by the few schools and colleges they attended, for e.g., Eton and Harrow, Oxford and Cambridge. Note that in cricket, it is no longer gentleman versus player—there are no gentlemen left, or, as we all say proudly, we are all players now. Cricket teams around the world are composed of players who either speak English poorly or not at all. I grew up when cricket commentators spoke with beautiful accents and aristocratic players came with degrees from Oxbridge—e.g., Nawab of Pataudi of India and Imran Khan of Pakistan.

Education allows an increase in income and an increased ability to participate. What else can be more democratic?

A change in the elite in India

The single most critical factor in Indian politics, from its independence in 1947 until the birth of the Modi administration in 2014, was that the *same* elite ruled the country. Regardless of political affiliation, this elite had broadly the same political and economic philosophy, characterized by Western style social liberalism and Fabian economic socialism. In addition, this traditional elite was heavily anti-American.

In 2014, India, for the first time in its near seventy-year history changed and broadened its elite. Mr Modi is the son of a chaiwallah (a tea-seller); the previous elites and prime ministers were mostly upper class Hindus, and most belonged to the highest Brahmin caste.

What is noteworthy of the recent change in the elites is that Modi comes from the Bharatiya Janata Party (BJP), a party that was first in power at the national level from 1998 to 2004. Its leader and prime minister then was Atal Bihari Vajpayee, a very popular PM who continued to bring about changes in the economy engineered by the previous governments since 1991. However, Mr Vajpayee was very much a part of the same set of upper class values, beliefs and behaviour. The elite did not change under him—it was only the difference between Tweedledum and Tweedledee. With chaiwallah Modi there is a very distinct change in the style and content of leadership.

Economic policies in India under Modi have broadened the scope of action, mostly radical action. There is demonetization on the economic front—an upheaval which made illegal more than 85 per cent of currency notes in circulation. The old elite lost out—while they fought its insertion and implementation, the large masses of India gave Modi a thumbs up. Agriculture was a sector that the old elite were too elitist to reform—for the first time in seventy years, India is reforming the agricultural sector.

On the social side, there have been reforms heretofore ignored by the old elite. In his first Red Fort address on 15 August 2014, Prime Minister Modi condemned the predominantly North Indian practice of killing the girl child. In the same address, Modi talked about the scourge of open defecation, and the need for toilets for women (and now there is a Bollywood movie on the subject). Very recently, India finally passed a law against the anti-women Muslim religious practice of triple talaq—where a Muslim man could divorce his wife by just saying 'I divorce thee' three times, and be done. Why had the old elite not banned the practice of triple talaq? Not only did the old elite not do so (as most Muslim countries including Pakistan and Saudi Arabia had done), they introduced into law (by that icon of the old elite and scion of the Nehru–Gandhi dynasty, the late Rajiv Gandhi) an Act whereby the Muslim shouting *'Talaq, talaq, talaq'*, did not have to pay alimony. And why did the old elite (represented by the Congress party) do that? Because it wanted to win the Muslim vote.

The infamous alimony case in question—the 1978 Shah Bano case

Shah Bano, a sixty-two-year-old Muslim mother of five, was divorced by her husband. She filed and won the right to alimony from her Muslim husband.

With an overwhelming majority in Parliament, the Congress party, led by Rajiv Gandhi, reversed the Supreme Court judgement and denied Shah Bano the alimony that a uniform civil code would have allowed.

The Congress party passed the Muslim Women (Protection of Rights on Divorce) Act in 1986—a regressive law which restricted the right of Muslim divorcées to alimony from their former husbands for only ninety days after the divorce (the period of Iddah in Islamic Law).

India, at present, has laws that allow the adoption of different civil laws for different religions. Despite that, the Supreme Court has now ruled that 'triple talaq' is illegal. Next on the agenda will likely be the implementation of a uniform civil code. Indeed, if a uniform civil code had been present, non-democratic actions, like the Shah Bano judgement, could not have happened. And with a uniform civil code, it will be a new order.

By no means is it the case that what the new elite wants is 'good' or liberal (again, in the good sense!). In the new elite regime, anti-Muslim sentiment has been 'encouraged' via cow vigilantism.

The new elite slogan—'In the name of the cow'—has replaced the previous slogan of the old elite—'In the name of the poor'. Only while 'in the name of the poor' led to increased corruption, the cow has led to increased lynch deaths of innocent Muslims. Why and how? Because some members of the new elite feel emboldened by the Hindu majority (80+ per cent of the population) to not only ban the eating of beef but also lynch anyone they suspect (invariably a Muslim) of eating beef.

There are other tensions introduced by the new elite. In the name of nationalism (and irresponsible patriotism), the learned Supreme Court now requires all filmgoers to stand up for the national anthem played in every theatre before screening any movie in the land. I remember crying when the national anthem was played—now I cry for a different reason.

The new elite is a fact of life. Democracies and constitutions will have to find a way to convert the ugly inclinations of the new elite into less problematic practices, and over time, the bad will be minimized.

The Indian people are asking more questions and demanding greater accountability from dynastic political leaders. But the old elite—the politicians, the corporates, the left-intellectuals, the academics—cannot be expected to give up their privileges so easily. They will try to derail the transformation, object at every turn. If that means fake analysis, they will do so. If that means intellectual gymnastics, they will do so. The key point is that they *must* do so—it is a matter of self-preservation. It is another matter that they won't succeed.

This is a long-drawn-out battle, and a healthy battle, too. This is what checks and balances are all about. Should the new elite emerge without being questioned? Absolutely not. Can the new elite just be allowed to roll over the old elite? Definitely not. Will the old elite use all its instruments and cash in all the old I-owe-you(s) in order to influence the debate with fake news and even flakier analysis if need be? You bet.

India is going through this transition. Make no mistake about it—other countries will follow for much the same reason—the expansion of the educated middle class. In non-democratic societies, the new educated elite will bring liberal progress in the form of increased openness and enhanced rights, especially for women. In already democratic societies like India, the transition to a more democratic society will involve some costs.

This is one movie we have never seen before. But we will see several replays over the next decade, in different locales. Sit back, learn, comprehend, and enjoy.

13

You Can't Fool Mother Nature

At first I was afraid, I was petrified, ...
And so you're back from outer space , ...
Go on now, go. Walk out the door ...
Did you think I'd crumble?
Did you think I'd lay down and die?
Oh, no, not I!
I will survive.

—I Will Survive *by* Gloria Gaynor
(*lyrics by* Freddie Perren and Dino Fekaris, Love Tracks, 1978)

It is one of the great iconic ads, and one with a universal and age-old lesson. The year was 1971. New technology—biotech—was beginning to flex its muscles. Forever, we have believed that we can change the course of nature. That somehow, with the right mix of policy and endeavour, we can change the inevitable. But more on this later.

Truly this is the age of revolution. The world has been turned upside down and sideways, and it is still changing and evolving. Yesterday's core is tomorrow's periphery. Merely ten years ago, it was very different, and just twenty-five years ago, it was ancient. What changed in such a short time period? To be sure, the communications revolution has something to do with it. But it is the unprecedented expansion of education in developing countries, especially in China and India, which is responsible for the changed world today.

Both these large economies have grown rather well over the last thirty-odd years. President Trump believes he can make America great *again*. Maybe he feels that America is no longer great because it is not growing as fast as China or India. The emphasis on 'again' implies that America was once great, but has now fallen on hard times. The result of our discussions on the transformative force of education suggests that Trump is wrong on at least two counts. First, that America is no longer great. Second, that somehow, with his mix of policies on immigration, he can change the future course of events.

America the Great

First things first. No matter what the criteria, America is great today, and has been for at least the last 200 years. We had noted how possibly because of its egalitarian emphasis and pursuit of education for all, it wrested the mantle of the richest country from England in the mid-19th century, and this at a time when the colonial empire was at its peak. America is great because, in relative terms, it is better than most societies on this collective broad criteria—democracy, individual rights, less racism, less discrimination, and high per capita income. But Trump may have a point to make: how can a country be great with a dysfunctional medical care system? To the best of my understanding, President Trump's new greatness policies will make matters worse.

Getting back to Mother Nature, Trump believes that by building a wall and restricting immigration he can make US wages rise at a faster pace. In Chapter 7, we had noted how the expansion of educational attainments in the developing world had 'robbed' America and other Western nations of the greatness associated with high rates of wage growth. 'Make America great again' is meant to resonate with the crackle associated with industry. But Mother Nature long ago suggested that the road to nirvana was not painted with industry. Services perhaps. Maybe technology or maybe even software. First industry moved eastward, and now software services are doing so. But artificial intelligence, 3D printing, and technology yet unseen are on their way—factors that are bound to keep America great for a long time.

But will building the wall or restricting immigration help in any way increase the rate of growth of the wages of American workers—a rate of growth that has averaged less than a 10 per cent aggregate increase since the turn of the century? Note that the job expansion that has occurred in the US in the last several years has been unprecedented in its scope—the unemployment rate is at its lowest, and that too, on a sustained basis. But the trend in wages is one of a slow increase, and much slower than ever before. The only way that this trend in US wages can be arrested is if the US stops all trade. And economists have a very good idea of what that will do to US living standards—the road to hell is a steep fall when you ignore Mother Nature.

Let me make a confession—I come from India, a country that has systematically ignored the market (nature) for most of its seventy-year existence. In India, profit has been a four-letter word; thankfully, this 'elite' concept is now going the way of the dinosaur.

Basic income for the bottom 50 per cent

Mother Nature has provided us with a new dilemma. We know that markets work, and we know that they don't necessarily yield a desirable outcome vis-à-vis distribution. Imagine a world where everybody broadly has the same level of education. It is not a utopia I am talking about; it is the present-day reality in the Western world. There is education inequality in the West, but broadly of an irreducible nature. There are other determinants of income—hard work, motivation, entrepreneurship, and one's innate ability. In the limit, it is ability that will drive income inequality. If the Western economies are any guide (yes, the Western world is more than the US), then inequality is likely to *decline* in the future. Ascribe it to Mother Nature if you will, but ability seems to have less inequality than aggregate income.

But there is a Mother Nature problem that societies will have to face and resolve. There will be people left behind. Just look at the Charlottesville white Americans and the brown gau rakshaks (cow vigilantes) in India. Is there a difference? None whatsoever. Both are predominantly, almost exclusively male. Both have less than the average level of education. Both (likely, and here I am indulging in informed speculation) have seen their spouses perform better than them in the marketplace, which only enhances their sense of insecurity.

It is true that women have taken a secondary role for a long time and have (usually) not resorted to antisocial behaviour—nor are they expected to do so in the future. But society needs to recognize that there may be reasons (unemployment, insecurity) for antisocial behaviour among men. Lack of adequate income is one such reason that societies can do something about.

In Chapter 9, we had discussed that basic income is an age-old idea, tried first in England in the 18th century. Switzerland recently had a referendum on the provision of a basic income to all the residents. It was defeated. But the likelihood of basic income reappearing in a format that is not for the entire population but for the bottom half or bottom third is high. And not just in Switzerland but across the world. Don't fight the irresistible force of Mother Nature—it often means well.

*

Like the crowd in Shakespeare's *Julius Caesar*, you are clamouring for the ad—the ad, the ad. In 1971, a biotech firm believed that it had beaten Mother Nature by manufacturing something that tastes just like butter, but isn't butter—it's margarine. Mother Nature is given butter, sorry margarine, to taste, and she pronounces it as delicious and buttery. But then she is told that it is not butter. Mother Nature is then upset, there is lightning, and she snorts, 'It is not *nice* to fool Mother Nature'. As margarine found out a couple of decades later, Mother Nature had the last word. She was right, it is not nice to fool her—just ask Chiffon margarine. It is no more, and butter reigns supreme.

The final word

The point about Mother Nature is obviously one of inevitability and the fact that its force is supreme. The force of education is a force of nature—it changes life, habits, societies, elites. Let us just look back at what education has made possible, and then debate whether it is not the second greatest force in history, after Mother Nature.

If technology is the buzzword, it was made possible by the educated, now more numerous. Ditto with artificial intelligence—the new buzz in the block—and with the atom bomb and weapons of mass destruction.

Yes, this is the story of the good and the ugly. The ugly, we all know. I want to just summarize the sweeping good. Greater equality in incomes, a democratization of the elite, economic growth and better standards of living, the elimination of poverty, and the equality of sexes. All made possible by the force of education, the new wealth of nations.

Notes

1. All data on education is sourced from Barro-Lee (2015). See Chapter 3 for details.

2. The fact that many countries have adopted inflation targeting since the mid-1990s—almost to the day since the reality of constant real wages—illustrates how economists are often the last to see the reality of their handiwork and their insights. Spare a tear for India, a country that adopted inflation targeting in 2016, literally after the inflation horse had bolted.

3. The West consists of the Western world, including Japan, i.e., the so called Advanced Economies (AEs). Sometimes, particularly for the period prior to 1950, the West also refers to the countries belonging to the former Soviet Union. East, Rest, developing economies, and emerging markets are broadly interchangeable descriptions of non-Western economies.

4. Sourced from World Economic Outlook, IMF (2017); see Chapter 3 for a discussion about sources and methods of computation; also see Bhalla (2002) and Bhalla (2007), two earlier works on global income distribution, etc.

5. For our analysis of distribution, we use the Piketty's WID.world data, when available. The WID data 'adjusts' official household data for the top 5 to 10 per cent of the population, and does so via the use of income tax data.

6. See Bhalla (2004), Bhalla (2007).

7. Tiger Mom is used for describing a tough, disciplinarian mother—following the book *Battle Hymn of the Tiger Mother* by Amy Chua who describes bringing up her children in the strict, traditional Chinese way.

8. Numbers obtained from US Electoral College archives which can be accessed at https://www.archives.gov/federal-register/electoral-college/historical.html.

9. Two Latin phrases are critical for any conversation among economists—*ceteris paribus*, meaning all other things being equal (which of course they never are), and *mutatis mutandis*, which means when all other things are allowed to change. In keeping with tradition, and in the interest of saving space, we will use these phrases in the text.

10. An earlier version of these calculations was reported in my 2002 book, *Imagine There's No Country*.

11. The calculation of income gains according to household surveys are problematic because of radically different kinds of 'income capture' either for the same country over time, or for different countries at a point in time. For e.g., the household consumption survey in India, the primary source for inferences about poverty and inequality, was able to capture less than 50 per cent of the consumption of all households; in contrast, the survey capture in China is upwards of 80 per cent.

12. Maddison (2001, 2003 and 2006).

13. The latest such estimates are provided for 2011. The question the data answers is the following: in 2011, what did an identical basket of goods and services cost in different countries? The currency of exchange is the PPP and the year of valuation is 2011. This PPP exchange rate is then extended forwards and backwards based on differences in inflation rates relative to the US. So whenever you see the notification in '2011 PPP' prices, that is what the author

is referring to. One additional point regarding data: the 2011 PPP data for India and China was not accepted by many economists, including Maddison. We follow the practice of Piketty et al. in using the Maddison adjusted PPP data for India and China.

14. Cross-country data post-1950 is available in two parts, 1950–1979, and 1980–present, and besides this there are data estimates for the future. The 1950–1979 country level economic data is available from the detailed and pioneering set of calculations contained in the Penn Tables, which, in turn, contain Maddison's estimates. Post-1979, the official keeper of the data is the IMF. This data was used by me in 2002 in constructing world economy (distribution and poverty) estimates reported in *Imagine There's No Country* and has been updated for this book.

15. a) The analysis of country-wise individual and world inequality was first presented in Bhalla (2002); the methodology of computing inequality followed the procedure outlined in Kakwani (1980). In a review of the various world inequality analyses that have proliferated since 2002, Darvas (2016) considers the Kakwani procedure to be the most accurate.

   b) All inequality data incorporates the WID (World Inequality Database) for the Piketty type adjustments to income inequality for the top 10 per cent, the top 5 per cent and the top 1 per cent of the populations in the different countries.

16. Perhaps, not coincidentally, since Williamson (2006) dedicated the book to Arthur Lewis, Moses Abramovitz and Bertil Ohlin.

17. The Caribbean islands did not gain independence till the middle of the 20th century (Jamaica in 1962, Barbados in 1966).

18. These tabulations exclude those countries which were colonies before and are now part of the developed world, for e.g., the USA, Canada, etc.

19. Report published by Freedom House.

20. See Bhalla (2015) for details.

21. Coincidentally, projections suggest that by 2025, the two countries will have equal populations—both around 1450 million.

22. The smallest country in 2016 was Palau in East Asia, with a population of 21,502. The crossover country for India's 1.3 billion population is Iraq (population: 37 million) and the crossover country for China's population of 1410 million is Algeria (population: 41.3 million). It takes 119 countries to reach the 328 million population size of the USA.

23. The issue of the same political union is more of a debatable question in India than in China. While it's understandable that this debate should occur, a divergence (now) made famous by Amartya Sen's *The Argumentative Indian*, the truer story is that, like China, India has also been a loose political union for most part of the past thousand years, and before.

24. Based on data compiled by Barro and Lee (2015). Also, for the US, see Goldin and Katz (2008).

25. See Goldin and Katz (2008) for a detailed discussion on educational expansion in the US.

26. The concepts of the emerging middle class and the middle class are discussed in Chapter 11; also see Kaur (2014). The formulation of the lines (incomes) separating the poor from the middle class, etc. are based on PPP data, comparable across space and time. I was born in an emerging middle class family by world standards, but a classic middle class family by Indian standards.

27. The relationship between R^2 and t-statistic is equivalent to the relationship between mutatis mutandis and ceteris paribus!

28. The t-statistic is a statistical measure which summarizes the 'tightness of fit'. For e.g., a low t-value, say less than 1.8, could also be explained by 'noise' or by factors other than those being considered in the model; a high t-value, especially above 2, is considered to pass the 'Good Housekeeping' test of statistical significance. Incidentally, a t-statistic of 1.96 implies that one

would be making a false association or dependence 5 per cent of the time.

29. However, the availability of detailed data on education, for e.g., Barro-Lee, is beginning to make a dent; see Manuelli–Seshadri (2014), Jones (2014).

30. Ashenfelter was my PhD thesis adviser in the Economics Department at Princeton University. He was described by Angus Maddison as 'a genius who looks like a truck driver'. One of the reasons for my continued and endearing friendship with Orley was the fact that he was able to perfectly imitate an Indian accent—something, unfortunately, today's charged atmosphere of political correctness does not allow.

31. The adjustment factor here is the PPP/US$ ratio (for India and China in 1996, the values are 0.26 and 0.34 respectively).

32. Bhalla (2017a) contains details for measuring educational wealth for different years from 1870 to 2016, and projections till 2030.

33. To reiterate, the real exchange rate is measured as the ratio of the PPP exchange rate to the US dollar exchange rate. When this ratio is more than 1, it is assumed to be 1, which is the real exchange rate for the US. In other words, by definition, no country has a superior education quality than the US.

34. See Thomas et al (2000) for one of the earliest documentations of Education Gini at both country and world level. Our estimates are different (and much higher) because of our attempt at quality adjustment via the real exchange rate.

35. Econometric details are presented in Bhalla (2017b); also see Autor–Katz–Kearney (2005), Goldin–Katz (2008) and Edwards–Lawrence (2013).

36. See Golob (1994) and Bordo (2000).

37. Unless otherwise stated, in this chapter the West refers to the AEs plus the countries belonging to Eastern Europe and the former Soviet Union.

38. Given that men have been in dominant control forever, why is it that nature, the greatest force, is not referred to as Father Nature? Did the men who coined the phrase have a premonition about the emerging reality, albeit one that would emerge over a thousand years later?

39. Again, Becker (1957) is responsible for the introduction of the 'economics of discrimination'.

40. The probability of a boy being born is 51.25 per cent and this means that the probability of a girl birth is 48.75 per cent. The ratio of the two (multiplied by 100) is the sex ratio at birth—105.3.

41. See Kaur et al (2016) who contend that normality in sex ratio at birth will return to India, at an aggregate level, by 2025.

42. See Chapter 3 for details on the construction of Income Distribution data.

43. Mea Culpa. I wrote a paper for the World Bank (Bhalla, 1978) showing that if the data were assembled correctly, it would show that there was a worsening of income inequality in South Korea during the period 1965–1975. But how much had inequality worsened? By a miniscule 5 per cent. What was 'important', however, was to show that growth was not accompanied by an improving income distribution, as some had argued. Whether this was political correctness or a desire to show that the Kuznets Curve held is unclear. What is clear, with hindsight, is that South Korean income distribution has not only not worsened but improved with growth, and the Kuznets Curve works very rarely, even in the medium term, say five to fifteen years.

44. See Bhalla (2002) for an extended discussion and summary of the available evidence.

45. See Thomas et al (2001) on how to generate the Gini from grouped Barro-Lee data on education—grouped by illiteracy (zero schooling), primary school attendance, primary school completion, etc.

46. Giving credit where it is due: Shekhar Gupta, a good friend and former editor of *Indian Express*, the leading English language daily in India, and for which I have been a contributing editor for nearly ten years, is the 'owner' of the term 'povertarian'. While we are dropping names, etc., let me just add that the now everyday phrase in India, 'in the name of the poor', has my copyright! In an article published in the mid-1980s, I coined the secular phrase Bis-mil-Muflis or 'I begin in the name of the poor'—secular because poverty is the only equivalence among all religions. To prove the point that there are many authors to a phrase, Bis-mil-Muflis was created (for me) by another good friend, Saeed Naqvi, one of India's top journalists.

47. See Kaur (2014), *The Emerging Middle Class.*

48. A simple regression of fraction of poor on fraction of illiterates yields the result that each 1 per cent decline in illiteracy results in a 0.83 per cent decline in absolute poverty.

49. See Lawrence, Robert Z. *The Diminishing Role of Manufacturing as a Source of Inclusive Growth: The Experience of Emerging Economies.*

50. In 1991, Vinod Thomas led the team writing the World Bank's *World Development Report 1991: The Challenge of Development.* The WDR team commissioned a project to assemble data on primary, secondary, and tertiary school enrolments for developing countries. The team that assembled the data included Lawrence Lau, Frederic Luoat, and I. So my association with education data is old, quite old.

51. Homi (also a close friend) and I can take credit for coming up with the first published middle class line. In 1991, we wrote a paper for the World Bank outlining the poverty and middle class line for Malaysia; I extended the definition for the world in my 2002 book, *Imagine There's No Country.* The 2007 definition and the 2017 definition are the same—the poverty line in advanced economies.

Select Bibliography

Alan Heston, Robert Summers and Bettina Aten. 2002. 'Penn World Table Version 6.3.' Center for International Comparisons at the University of Pennsylvania (CICUP), August.

Alesina, Alberto and Eliana La Ferrara. 2004. 'Ethnic Diversity and Economic Performance.' NBER Working Paper, no. 10313, November.

Alvaredo, Facundo, Anthony B. Atkinson, Emmanuel Saez and Thomas Piketty. 2015. The World Wealth & Incomes Database.

Anand, Sudhir and Ravi Kanbur. 1993. 'The Kuznets Process and the Inequality–Development Relationship.' *Journal of Development Economics* 40, no. 1: 25–52, June.

Anesi, George. 2003. 'Private Property and the Rule of the Middle Class in Aristotle's Politics.' *Draft, Classics of Social and Political Thought*. Department of Social Sciences, University of Chicago, November.

Ashenfelter, Orley and Joseph D. Mooney. 1968. 'Graduate Education, Ability, and Earnings.' *The Review of Economics and Statistics* 50, no. 1: 78–86.

Asian Development Bank. 2002. *Asian Drama Re-visited: Policy Implications for the Poor*. Report prepared for research project RETA-5917 by a team led by Surjit S. Bhalla.

Autor, David H., Lawrence F. Katz and Melissa S. Kearney. 2005. 'Rising

Wage Inequality: The Role of Composition and Prices.' NBER Working Paper, no. 11628, September.

Banerjee, Abhijit and Thomas Piketty. 2005. 'Top Indian Incomes, 1922–2000.' *The World Bank Economic Review* 19, no. 1: 1–20.

Barro, Robert J. and Jong-Wha Lee. 2013. 'A New Data Set of Educational Attainment in the World, 1950-2010.' *Journal of Development Economics* 104: 184–198.

_____.2015. *Education Matters: Global Schooling Gains from the 19th to the 21st century*. New York: Oxford University Press.

Becker, Gary S. 1957. *The Economics of Discrimination* (2nd Edition). Chicago: University of Chicago Press.

_____.1960. 'An Economic Analysis of Fertility.' *Demographic and Economic Change in Developed Countries*. New Jersey: Princeton University Press for NBER.

_____.1962. 'Investment in Human Capital: A Theoretical Analysis.' *Journal of Political Economy* 70, no. 5, Part 2: 9–49.

_____.1964. *Human Capital: A Theoretical and Empirical Analysis, With Special Reference to Education*. Chicago: University of Chicago Press.

_____.1965. 'A Theory of the Allocation of Time.' *The Economic Journal*: 493–517.

_____.2009. *A Treatise on the Family*. Cambridge: Harvard University Press.

Becker, Gary S., and Barry R. Chiswick. 1966. 'Education and the Distribution of Earnings.' *The American Economic Review* 56, no. 1/2: 358–369.

Becker, Gary S., and Nigel Tomes. 1979. 'An Equilibrium Theory of the Distribution of Income and Intergenerational Mobility.' *Journal of Political Economy* 87, no. 6: 1153–1189.

Bernanke, Ben S. 2005. *The Global Saving Glut and the U.S. Current Account Deficit*, no. 77.

Bhalla, Surjit S. 1973. 'The Education-Income Connection: An

Investigative Report.' New Jersey: Princeton University. Available at https://www.princeton.edu/rpds/papers/WP_40.pdf.

———.1996. 'This Time it is Different.' Deutsche Bank. New York. Available at https://ssbhalla.files.wordpress.com.

———.1997a. 'Freedom and Economic Growth: A Virtuous Cycle?' In *Democracy's Victory and Crisis*, ed. Axel Hadenius. Cambridge: Cambridge University Press.

———.1997b. 'Social Justice: Educate Little Girls'. *Economic Times*, April 30.

———.2000. 'Bis-mil-muflis: In the Name of the Poor.' *Business Standard*, 16 September.

———.2002. *Imagine There's No Country: Poverty, Inequality and Growth in the Era of Globalization*. Washington: Institute of International Economics.

———.2004. 'Poor Result and Poorer Policy: A Comparative Analysis of Estimates of Global Inequality and Poverty.' *CESifo Economic Studies* 50, no.1/2004: 85–132.

———.2006a. 'This Time It is Different: India at a Structural Break.' Toyota, 14 November. Tokyo.

———.2006b. 'Comments on Richard Freeman, Labour Market Imbalances: Shortages or Surpluses, or Fish Stories.'

———.2007. 'Second Among Equals: The Middle Class Kingdoms of India and China.' Peterson Institute of International Economics, Washington. May (Photocopy). Available at https://ssbhalla.files.wordpress.com/2015/08/second_among_equals_-_omega_august-25-2015.pdf.

———.2012. *Devaluing to Prosperity: Misaligned Currencies and Their Growth Consequence*. New Delhi: Oxford University Press.

———.2015. 'Democracy Growth and Development in India: 1951-2012.' In *India and the Pursuit of Inclusive Growth,* eds Anne Applebaum and Ann Bernstein. Centre for Development and Enterprise, and Legatum Institute. Available at http://www.cde.org.za/india-and-the-pursuit-of-inclusive-growth/.

———.2016. 'Food, Hunger and Nutrition in India: A Case of Redistributive Failure.' Report to Brookings Institution. Available at https://ssbhalla.files.wordpress.com/2016/02/food-hunger-and-nutrition-in-india-a-case-of-redistributive-failure.pdf.

———.2017a. 'Towards Estimation of Education Wealth.' Available at https://ssbhalla.files.wordpress.com/.

———.2017b. 'College Wages in the US and Global Labour Supply.' Available at https://ssbhalla.files.wordpress.com/.

Bhalla, Surjit S. and Homi Kharas. 1991. Chapters on 'Growth, Poverty Alleviation and Improved Income Distribution in Malaysia: Changing Focus of Government Policy Intervention.' World Bank Report 8667. Washington: World Bank.

Bhalla, Surjit S., Suraj Saigal, Nabhojit Basu. 2003. 'Girl's Education Is It—Nothing Else Matters (Much)'. Washington, DC: World Bank. Available at: http://documents.worldbank.org/curated/en/502101468771256653/Girls-education-is-it-nothing-else-matters-much

Bordo, Michael D. 2000. 'Sound money and sound financial policy.' *Journal of Financial Services Research* 18, no. 2–3: 129–155.

Bourguignon, François and Christian Morrisson. 2002. 'Inequality among World Citizens: 1820–1992.' *American Economic Review*, September.

Brian, Eric and Marie Jaisson. 2007. *The Descent of Human Sex Ratio at Birth: A Dialogue between Mathematics, Biology and Sociology* (Volume 4). Springer Science & Business Media.

Chancel, Lucas and Thomas Piketty. 2017. 'Indian income inequality, 1922-2014: From British Raj to Billionaire Raj?' WID.world Working Paper Series. Available at http://wid.world/document/chancelpiketty2017widworld/.

Chua, Amy. 2011. *Battle Hymn of the Tiger Mother*. Penguin.

Clark, Gregory. 2005. 'Human capital, fertility, and the industrial revolution.' *Journal of the European Economic Association* 3, no. 2–3: 505–515.

Credit Suisse Research Institute. 2016. 'Global Wealth Report.'

Darvas, Zsolt. 2016. 'Some are More Equal than Others: New Estimates of Global and Regional Inequality.' Bruegel Working Papers.

David, H., Lawrence F. Katz and Melissa S. Kearney. 2005. 'Trends in US Wage Inequality: Re-Assessing the Revisionists.' National Bureau of Economic Research, no. w11627.

Deaton, Angus. 2013. *The Great Escape: Health, Wealth, and the Origins of Inequality*. Princeton University Press.

Edwards, Lawrence, and Robert Z. Lawrence. 2013. *Rising Tide: Is Growth in Emerging Economies Good for the United States?* Washington DC: Peterson Institute for International Economics.

Fischer, Stanley. 2017. *The Low Level of Global Real Interest Rates: a speech at the Conference to Celebrate Arminio Fraga's 60 Years,* Casa das Garcas, no. 966, Rio de Janeiro, 31 July.

Forbes. 2017. *The World's Billionaires.*

Franck, Raphaël, and Oded Galor. 2015. *Industrialization and the Fertility Decline.* Working Paper, no. 2015–6. Department of Economics, Brown University.

Freedom House. 2017. *Freedom in the World.*

Freeman, Richard. 2005. 'China, India and the Doubling of the Global Labor Force: who pays the price of globalization?' *The Globalist.*

Freund, Caroline. 2016. *Rich People Poor Countries: The Rise of Emerging-Market Tycoons and their Mega Firms.* Washington DC: Peterson Institute for International Economics.

Goldhammer, Arthur, et al. 2017. *After Piketty: The Agenda for Economics and Inequality,* ed. Heather Boushey, J. Bradford Delong and Marshall Steinbaum. Cambridge: Harvard University Press.

Goldin, Claudia Dale, and Lawrence F. Katz. 2009. *The Race between Education and Technology: The Evolution of U.S. Educational Wage Differentials, 1890 to 2005.* Cambridge: Harvard University Press.

Golob, John E. 1994. 'Does Inflation Uncertainty Increase with Inflation?' *Economic Review-Federal Reserve Bank of Kansas City* 79, no. 3: 27.

Hause, John C. 1975. 'Ability and Schooling as Determinants of Lifetime Earnings, or If You're So Smart, Why Aren't You Rich?' *Education, Income, and Human Behavior NBER*: 123–150.

Isaksson, Anders. 2007. 'World Productivity Database: A Technical Description.' RST Staff Working Paper 10. Vienna: UNIDO.

James, Lawrence. 2006. *The Middle Class: A History*. London: Little Brown.

Jones, Benjamin F. 2014. 'The Human Capital Stock: A Generalized Approach.' *American Economic Review* 104, no. 11: 3752–3777.

Judson, Ruth. 1996. *Do Low Human Capital Coefficients Make Sense? A Puzzle and Some Answers*. Federal Reserve Board, Division of Research and Statistics, Division of Monetary Affairs.

Juselius, Mikael and Előd Takáts. 2015. 'Can Demography Affect Inflation and Monetary Policy?' Bank of International Settlements Working Papers, no. 485.

Kaur, Ravinder. 2014. 'The 'Emerging' Middle Class: Role in the 2014 General Elections.' *Economic and Political Weekly* 49, no. 26–27, 28 June.

Kaur, Ravinder, et al. 2017. *Sex Ratio at Birth: The Role of Gender, Class and Education*. United Nations Population Fund. Available at http://india.unfpa.org/sites/default/files/pub-pdf/Sex%20 Ratio%20at%20Birth%20-%20Revised_1.pdf.

Kuznets, Simon. 1955. 'Economic growth and income inequality.' *The American Economic Review* 45, no. 1: 1–28.

Lawrence, Robert Z. Mimeo. 'The Diminishing Role of Manufacturing as a Source of Inclusive Growth: The Experience of Emerging Economies.' Phase Three Report: Manufacturing as a Source of Inclusive Growth. MasterCard Center for Inclusive Growth.

Lewis, Sir William Arthur. 1954. 'Economic Development with Unlimited Supplies of Labour.' *The Manchester School* 22, no. 2: 139–191.

———.1978. *The Evolution of the International Economic Order (Eliot*

Janeway Lectures on Historical Economics in Honor of Joseph Schumpeter). Princeton University Press.

Lindert, Peter H. 2000. 'Three Centuries of Inequality in Britain and America.' *Handbook of Income Distribution* 1: 167–216.

Luxembourg Income Study (LIS) Database. *http://www.lisdatacenter.org* (multiple countries). Luxembourg.

Luxembourg Wealth Study (LWS) Database. *http://www.lisdatacenter. org* (multiple countries). Luxembourg.

Maddison, Angus. 2001. *The World Economy: A Millennial Perspective.* Paris: Organization for Economic Cooperation and Development.

_____.2003. *The World Economy: Historical Statistics.* Paris: Organization for Economic Cooperation and Development.

_____.2006. 'Asia in the world economy 1500–2030 AD.' *Asian–Pacific Economic Literature* 20, no. 2: 1–37.

Manuelli, R.E., and A. Seshadri. 2014. 'Human Capital and the Wealth of Nations.' *American Economic Review* 104, no. 9: 2736–2762.

Moore, Barrington. 1967. *Social Origins of Dictatorship and Democracy: Lord and Peasant in the Making of the Modern World.* Boston: Beacon Press.

Myrdal, Gunnar. 1968. *Asian Drama: An Inquiry into the Poverty of Nations.* New York: Pantheon.

Ogilvy & Mather. 2016. 'The Velocity 12 Markets: Reshaping the World View of Middle Class Growth.'

O'Neill, June. 2003. 'The Gender Gap in Wages, circa 2000.' *The American Economic Review* 93, no. 2: 309–314.

Oxfam. 2017. '*An Economy for the 99%.*' January.

Piketty, Thomas and Emmanuel Saez. 2003. 'Income inequality in the United States, 1913–1998.' *The Quarterly Journal of Economics*, 118(1): 1–41.

Piketty, Thomas. 2014. *Capital in the Twenty-First Century.* Cambridge: Harvard University Press.

Polanyi, Karl. 1944. *The Great Transformation: Economic and Political Origins of our Time.* New York: Rinehart & Company, Inc.

Psacharopoulos, George and Ana Maria Arriagada. 1986. 'The Educational Composition of the Labour Force: An International Comparison.' *International Labour Review* 125, no. 5: 561–574, September–October.

Rawls, John. 2009. *A Theory of Justice*. Cambridge: Harvard University Press.

Robinson, Joan. 1965. *Essays in the Theory of Economic Growth*. Macmillan.

Sen, Amartya. 1999. *Development as Freedom* (1st edition). New York: Oxford University Press.

Schoellman, Todd. 2012. 'Education Quality and Development Accounting.' *Review of Economic Studies* 79, no. 1: 388–417.

Stolper, Wolfgang and Paul A. Samuelson. 1941. 'Protection and Real Wages.' *Review of Economic Studies* 9, no.1: 58–73.

Sullivan, Eileen P. 1981. 'A Note on the Importance of Class in the Political Theory of John Stuart Mill.' *Political Theory* 9, no. 2: 248–256.

Summers, Lawrence H. 2014. 'US Economic Prospects: Secular Stagnation, Hysteresis, and the Zero Lower Bound.' *Business Economics* 49, no. 2: 65–73.

The World Bank. 1991. *World Development Report 1991: The Challenge of Development*. New York: Oxford University Press. Available at https://openknowledge.worldbank.org/handle/10986/5974.

_____.2017. World Development Indicators.

Thomas, Vinod, Yan Wang and Xibo Fan. 2001. *Measuring Education Inequality: Gini Coefficients of Education*, vol. 2525. World Bank Publications.

United Nations Development Programme (UNDP). 1990. *Human Development Report*. New York: Oxford University Press.

Vogel, Ezra F. 2013. *Deng Xiaoping and the Transformation of China*. Cambridge: Belknap Press of Harvard University Press.

Wealth-X. 2017. *World Ultra Wealth Report*.

Whalley, John and Xiliang Zhao. 2010. 'The Contribution of Human Capital to China's Economic Growth.' NBER Working Paper, no. 16592, December.

Whalley, John. 1979. 'The Worldwide Income Distribution: Some Speculative Calculations.' *Review of Income and Wealth* 25: 261–276.

Williamson, Jeffrey G. 2005. 'Globalization, de-industrialization and underdevelopment in the third world before the modern era.' IFCS—Working Papers in Economic History. WH. dilf0506, Universidad Carlos III de Madrid. Instituto Figuerola.

_____.2006. *Globalization and the Poor Periphery before 1950*. Cambridge: MIT Press.

Yoon, Mr Jong-Won, Mr Jinill Kim and Jungjin Lee. 2014. *Impact of Demographic Changes on Inflation and the Macroeconomy* (no. 14–210). International Monetary Fund.

ACKNOWLEDGEMENTS

Research is the thrill of discovery, and that explains why this book is not about what it was originally meant to be—an expanded, improved, and updated version of my 2007 manuscript *Second among Equals—The Middle Class Kingdoms of India and China*. The measurement of the size of the middle class and its influence on policy and growth by researchers and institutions has increased manifold since 2007. A decade later seemed like a perfect time to review, evaluate, and update.

I happened to be in the quiet, sleepy German town of Bielefeld, where Ravinder Kaur was teaching a short, intensive course on Gender, Technology, and Society. Bielefeld reminded me a lot of my own university town in the mid-1960s—Purdue University, West Lafayette, Indiana, in the middle of the Bible Belt, in the middle of nowhere, in the middle of mid-Western America—but a perfect place for education and thinking. She was teaching a class, I was working on my middle class book.

However, progress was slow, the writing difficult. Call it a writer's block or a lack of inspiration. Much as I wanted to get my middle class story on the cover of *Rolling Stone*—I hear that the magazine is up for sale—I was not able to get terribly excited about dwelling on that ten-year journey. Instead, I found true excitement in revisiting my journey since childhood.

Thought fermented around the things that tied together my research and policy interests—poverty, the middle class, development, the elite, joblessness...democracy, economic growth, and wealth. Finally, the Eureka moment! It all seemed to be inextricably tied with education.

There have been several markers in the intellectual journey that is contained in *The New Wealth of Nations*. It seems that forever I have been waiting to write about education. Indeed, my first ever 'publication' as a young graduate student in 1973 was a survey of the literature about the relationship between education and income. My contribution was labelling it as The Education–Income Connection, and Chapter 5 bears something of this title. (Any correlation with my film obsession and my fondness for thrillers is not coincidental—the movie *The French Connection* was released in 1971.) In 1974, I was awarded a pre-doctoral fellowship to the Brookings Institution; the subject of my proposed dissertation was: 'Inter-generational Inequality via Education'. I ended up writing my dissertation on another topic, but the interest has remained.

The editor at Simon and Schuster Dharini Bhaskar was tolerant enough to allow me extra time to finish. And thanks also to Dharini and Sayantan Ghosh for their suggestions and inputs towards transforming a quasi-academic subject into a (I hope successful) trade book!

There are various intellectual debts accumulated. I am lucky to have several close friends who have helped in this, and previous, discoveries. As every researcher knows, the exact origin of ideas is a broad unknown. Ravinder (also my wife) has argued, helped with intellectual inputs, sharpened my arguments, and kept me 'balanced' in my outlook and philosophy. If I am even half as helpful with her forthcoming book, I will consider that an achievement.

Suman Bery and Robert Lawrence have influenced my thinking and research in more ways than they give themselves credit (or blame) for. Homi Kharas, Farrukh Iqbal, and Arvind Virmani have been consistently generous with their time, arguments, and suggestions. And over the last few years, Josh Felman has been ever helpful with discussions. And all of them have sometimes—make that often—been too critical . . . but what else are friends for?

There are several other intellectual debts that need to be accounted for. I had worked on the Velocity 12 Project for Ogilvy & Mather, and I learnt a lot from Kent Wertime about the middle class and the sociology of development. I look forward to our joint work on the massive change in social life brought about by 'divorce', both individual and political.

Ruchir Sharma has led a self-styled gang of Limousine Liberals on election trips to different parts of India for the last twenty years. I have been a participant in many, and these trips have helped sharpen my analysis of development. Thank you, Ruchir, and I am dreading the day the team gets an election forecast wrong.

I have been an invitee since 2002 to the annual Aspen Program on the World Economy. Thanks, Bo Cutter, and especially for the discussions about politics, economics, and sports.

There are other debts. The Observatory Group has allowed me time to finish the book. More importantly, my analysis and my writing for a non-academic audience have improved enormously from my interaction with my editor-colleagues Ed Kean, Mary Rosenbaum, and Jin Saito.

There are yet other debts. Orley Ashenfelter, Alan Blinder, and George de Menil read through portions of the book (especially

Chapter 7), and while they are not responsible for the content, they are responsible for influencing my thinking. And Montek Ahluwalia has been doing so for the last 40+ years. Thank you.

While we are on the subject of thinking, the support of the family through discussions, intellectual inputs, arguments, disagreements, and agreements should not be underestimated. I'm indebted to Ravinder, Simran, and Sahil for being tolerant, and enabling, and feisty.

No long-run research is possible without the support of a team of research assistants. Over the years, I have benefitted from the support of Tirtha Das, Manoj Agrawal, Ankur Choudhary, Prasanthi Ramakrishnan, Rohini Sanyal, and Abhinav Motheram.

I have a DNA which is ++ and leads to an optimistic outlook (as testified by this book). Perhaps medical science will soon discover whether life's experiences lead to a ++ disposition or one's genes. *The New Wealth of Nations* is the product of research, experience, and maybe genes.